You and Your Life

Principles produce and increase the quality
of an excellent life

Winston Lucien Daniels

Order this book online at www.trafford.com
or email orders@trafford.com

Most Trafford titles are also available at major online book retailers.

Printed in the United States of America.

ISBN: 978-1-4269-3975-4 (sc)

Library of Congress Control Number: 2010911114

*Our mission is to efficiently provide the world's finest, most comprehensive book publishing
service, enabling every author to experience success. To find out how to publish your book, your
way, and have it available worldwide, visit us online at www.trafford.com*

Trafford rev. 08/24/2010

 www.trafford.com

North America & international
toll-free: 1 888 232 4444 (USA & Canada)
phone: 250 383 6864 ✦ fax: 812 355 4082

TABLE OF CONTENTS

Introduction

Have you ever heard this saying? 'An unexamined life is not worth living'? If not; please give careful attention to it. I know it is a hard thing to be nakedly honest about things that do not make us feel good about ourselves. Yet, these are the very things that limit and sabotage our great human potential. My encouragement is to face them head on. You are far bigger than anything bad that has ever happened to you. You are not that which has happened to you, rather, the true you has become limited by the bad experiences of life. Victory in all these unpleasant areas of life is vital to be able to enjoy good success in this world. You are weak in any area of past defeat in your life if you don't confront it head on. Your victory is based on your willingness to confront any such unpleasantness.

We do not all have the same understanding of how life works and of the many principles that govern it. Those who do have a deeper understanding can tap into an enriched and enjoyable life. Some of us have a mere primary understanding of life, just like a child at primary education level. Those of us who give attention to life and learn from every life experience are able to make a transition to a secondary understanding of life. Few of us have a tertiary understanding of life, though it is possible for anyone to progress this far. And very few of us reach a dimension of Mastery in which one begins to master all aspects of life no matter what happens. Any situation and circumstance can be converted into something good. That is mastery! I am not there yet; nevertheless, I had some foretaste of what it is. However, this foretaste is the software of that abundant life I am striving towards.

I am watching a television programme called "Starting Over" that gives the viewer finer insights into life by learning from other people's experiences. Reading biographies is also a very helpful tool to learn more about life from those who have lived enriched lives. Bible stories are equally important. Robert T. Kiyosaki, the author of 'Rich Dad Poor Dad' tells how his rich dad used Bible stories to teach his children about life and money. Whatever dimension or level you live your life from, will determine the quality of your life.

Where do you live - on a primary, secondary, tertiary or Mastery dimension? These dimensions give us an indication of the journey called life. My sincere encouragement is for you to upgrade yourself all the time by constantly improving your knowledge of life by giving close attention to anything that you experience in life, and learn from it. You cannot afford to make the same mistakes over and over – if you are making a mistake, let it be a new one, and learn from it.

You cannot enjoy life if you cannot manage your thought life and your emotional life. It is also very hard to enjoy life if you don't know yourself, and if you have a low self-esteem. Moreover, life will be even harder if you lack financial intelligence. Money plays a key role because it sustains life in many ways. Even the Bible says that money answers all things. These are some of the things I attempt to shed light on in this book. I hope I can give you some understanding of at least some of the things that pertain to life, so you can be enriched. Life is meant to be enjoyed; it is not about survival, not at all, but having said that, it is true that you can go on a survival course in the bush to help you learn some life skills.

Life my friend is in the NOW - we cannot live in the past, as we will be filled with a hopelessness, which will choke the life within us. Conversely, neither can we live in the future, as doing this will cause a deferred hope, making us sick at heart. The past does not equal the future; however your future unfolds day by day whilst you learn to live effectively in the NOW. Don't let what takes place in your 'now', pull you back into the past or cause you to daydream about a better future. Accept what is happening now, and find ways to work with it with a positive attitude until you get what it has to offer you. Your 'now' is called the present, which means it has presents (or gifts) to offer you! These presents come in disguised forms.

Concerning the future: It is true you must have a vision for your life, but you are not supposed to daydream about it all the time, unless it is constructive visualization coupled with action afterwards. You must have a vision for the future, but you must also rewind yourself back into your 'now' and do what needs to be done to manifest the future through daily action.

Whatever we focus on in life can either empower or disempower us. The truth is we tend to be more effective in focusing on what disempowers us. We tend to lack emotional strength, capacity and determination to focus on what can empower us. When we lack finances, we focus on lack instead of focusing on the fact that there is great abundance in the world. What we focus on can either work for us or against us. Do you know by focusing on the fact that there is abundance in the world you can, in fact, attract provision into your life? Perhaps you know by now that if you focus on lack, scarcity normally kicks in. Poverty kicks in when we dwell too long on scarcity. Do you normally focus on opportunities and possibilities, or risk and difficulty? Are you able to shift your focus from a negative thought to a more empowering thought? Have you noticed that you have a negative thought in your mind whenever you feel negative? Thoughts are highly energetic my friend, they produce feelings. I therefore beseech you to master the art of FOCUS. You cannot truly enjoy life if you do not have the capacity and strength to focus on something good when things are bad or something positive when things seem so negative in your life.

In conclusion: Please allow me to be your true friend as you read every single chapter in this book. I wrote this book for you! Who knows, we could meet some place where I am a guest speaker! Goals and focus have created a global village; small enough for us to bump into each other somewhere in this big world.

CHAPTER 1

LET'S TALK ABOUT LIFE

Life is the most precious gift to mankind from the most generous Author of life. What we do with the life we have received is our gift to the Author of life. There is therefore, more to life than just living and dying. Life is, what's happening to us, and it virtually becomes what we make happen.

I have come to the conclusion that life can be likened to a blank cheque, whatever we ask for is, in fact, what we write upon this most gracious cheque, and what we write tends to be revealed in its own timing. People, who ask little from life, get little, no doubt about it. Those who ask for much, tend to get much out of life. Life has no favourites, it treats everyone the same. Those who ask for nothing, get nothing. Our ability to ask for much is determined by our level of confidence and our confidence is determined by what we think, feel and say about ourselves. Confidence is the force behind achievements and accomplishments; we should therefore, not cast away our confidence, because therein lies our reward.

We are all born to succeed, since our Maker does not create failures, yet many of us do not really know this life-changing reality; therefore, we settle for failure, because there is a venture or ventures in our past which we perceive we have failed in. The truth is, we have labelled as failure that which was only a learning experience. 'Fail' means the **f**irst **a**ttempt **i**n **l**earning. Can you see that - **f**irst **a**ttempt **i**n **l**earning - is spelt **fail**? But you really did not fail. Go back to that event in your mind and in your heart and then take off that label and ask yourself what you can learn from it. Do not come back until you have found the valuable lesson that you are supposed to bring into another life experience. We learn more from what people call 'failure' than what we learn from success.

Success is sweet and it does not hurt, however, it is the very thing that hurts us that also teaches us valuable lessons. Do not be scared of pain – no pain, no gain. Pain is a driving force, and it is wisdom to relate pain to what does not work in life, in this way you will automatically move away from what is wrong, just like you would not put your hands on a hot stove.

Let's say you will only live until fifty years, and you are now twenty years old. Arise and shine my friend, because you only have thirty years left to make the most of your life. What about the person who is in his forties? You have ten years to make the most of your life. Age is only a number; it is how you feel about yourself that determines your real age. You only have one life to live. Make the most of your life by giving more attention to value-adding activities. Non value-adding activities are going-nowhere activities. It is a waste of life. Get actively involved in things that enable you to become a better person and improve the quality of your life. This is what you can give yourself – it is within your grasp.

HOW DO NON-VALUE-ADDING ACTIVITIES LOOK LIKE?

- Watching too much TV.

- Sitting or standing around doing nothing productive.

- Attending gossiping sessions with gossipers.

- Associating with people who are going nowhere in life. We become like our friends – this is called the power of association.

- Being critical, negative, judgmental, and faultfinding – these kinds of activities are a waste of time and energy.

- Allowing your past to control your current life. The past does not equal the future. Live life in the now.

- Wishful thinking and day dreaming about your future. Live life in the now. It is our daily activities that shape our future.

HOW DO VALUE-ADDING ACTIVITIES LOOK LIKE?

- Reading books that motivate and inspire.

- Listening to motivational teachings on CD.

- Listening to music that inspires.

- Attending workshops, seminars and conferences.

- Developing a gratitude attitude by keeping a gratitude journal.

- Study to show yourself approved in life.

- Associate with people who are wise and successful.

- Find ways how you can improve on your job or career.

- Do the things that make you feel good about yourself.

- Give yourself entirely to training and development for the rest of your life, it will keep you young and vibrant and passionate about life.

- Give constant attention to the renewing of your mind – read books that challenge your thinking.

- Give full attention to all areas that pertain to life – work on becoming a balanced person.

Live life to the fullest, because life has been made for you. It is meant to be enjoyed, avoid negativity at all cost, but deal with it positively whenever it happens to you. Don't be like most people who only see the negative when things are difficult. Diligently look for something positive in the situation to balance out the event. Don't walk away with negativity only. There is a blessing in every crisis and a positive in every negative situation. Furthermore, do not complain or blame even though you might be innocent. Complaining and blaming makes things worse, rather, choose to take full responsibility over the situation or circumstance. You are in command when you act responsibly, because by being responsible you will be elevated above your situation or circumstance. It empowers us to make things happen for ourselves and others. This is how you grow in becoming a leader. Leaders do the hard things that others shy away from. Hard things eventually become easy for them, because whatever we do consistently, becomes second nature, and second nature becomes first nature over time. Whatsoever becomes first nature adds to our capacity and weight. It is life-changing to be in the presence of a weighty person. Allow the storms of life to make you grow strong and stable. Ability flows out of stability.

Doubtless to say; life is very hard at times. Not accepting this reality makes life even harder. Accept the fact that life can be hard, because this reality produces a readiness in us to take responsibility, which releases our personal power to bring changes, find solutions or to simply endure the hard time graciously. So make things happen when life happens to be hard. Life also taught me that some things that seem to be hard are many times easy things that have been neglected. It is the little foxes that spoil the vines. We have to give each aspect of our lives a good amount of attention to get where we want to go in life. Life is on the move, it does not stand still for anyone.

Whatever we think, say and do is what we send out into life. Do not be deceived into thinking that you will get away with anything you think, say and do. It will return to you multiplied in mysterious ways. Whatever a man sows, that is what he will reap. The harvest of what we sow is always greater than the seed that we have sown. This is a law of life that can work against us, or for us. If we send out good all the time we will reap good all the time, which will set us up to live the good life. Why not use this law in your favor? Decide to send out good things consciously, everyday of your life. Send out smiles, friendliness, cheerfulness, joy, excitement, generosity, caring, compassion, forgiveness, help, assistance, support, mercy and grace all the days of your life and wait patiently to see how it returns to you in greater abundance. Furthermore, develop a consciousness of all the bad things that you unconsciously send out, call these bad 'seeds' back and cancel them. If necessary go and ask for forgiveness from those who have been affected by your bad attitudes, deeds and words. This kind of action will make a world of a difference in your life. It is a very empowering thing to ask for forgiveness.

Life is the biggest game ever played. It is the game that tends to produce very few champions simply because only a few of us give careful attention to life and make it our duty to study the rules that govern it. The rest of us fool ourselves into thinking we can break rules and get away with it. Breaking rules breaks us. Most of us are being played by life, while some of us only watch how others play life or how they are being played by life. Don't sit on the bench my friend – live life!

We have the power to choose – please choose life. Choose to become a player of life and learn to give attention to all areas of life and study the rules that govern it. You have the right to become a champion in life. Study to show yourself approved.

These are the eight areas of life:

- Spiritual
- Mental
- Emotional
- Physical (health and fitness)
- Family (spouse and children)
- Vocational
- Financial
- Social

You can be a winner in life by studying these eight areas of your life, and by setting yourself goals to become fulfilled in all of them. It is easy if you apply yourself diligently to each and every area. This book will give you a great kick-start.

CHAPTER 2

YOU AND YOUR LIFE

Our personal life consists of a deep inner life, a private life and a public life. You are a powerful human being if you can manage to create synergy between these three aspects of your life. This simply means to live in total harmony, allowing these three aspects to flow together and to work together as one. The very need to impress others is a sure sign that these three aspects of your life are incomplete. Powerful people impact others; they have no need to impress.

- **Our deep inner life** - this is where we connect with ourselves; ie. our thoughts, feelings, imaginings, experiences deep within and our deep inner beliefs. It includes our self-image, self-worth, self-esteem and our self-respect which can be either, an empowered or a disempowered sense of self and sense of right and wrong (conscience). In other words, our inner guidance – intuitive senses and our sensitivity to the Holy Spirit.

- **Our private life** – or personal life which may be lived alone, or with our spouse, family or close friends.

- **Our public life**, where we interact with people at our workplace or market place, at church, in our community and at social events.

Our most significant life is our deep inner life, with victory in this life preceding private victory, and private victory preceding public victory. Authenticity is when we truly live these three lives in total harmony. This means that I sincerely express myself to my family members in accordance with who I truly am within, and the person I am in my public life is exactly who I am at home.

Do you very best to be real to yourself and others. It makes life very easy and simple. Carrying a mask will drain you emotionally, since keeping a mask requires much energy and effort. This energy and effort could have been used to benefit you and others in many wonderful ways. The truth of the matter is, it is easier being your self than trying to be someone else. There is no need for two people in the same person.

CHAPTER 3

YOU AND YOUR POTENTIAL

There is no human being without great potential. Your lack of achievement and accomplishment says nothing about your potential. It does say that you have not yet tapped into your great human potential. Your potential is waiting to be used, released and maximized. A lack of achievement is a good indication that a person does not understand that he or she has potential and how it actually works. Anyone who understands how potential works will inevitably achieve his or her goals. Successful people are not special people, we are all special people. You too can become very, very successful if you want to.

DEFINING POTENTIAL:

I love definitions; they give a concise explanation of the meaning of a word, phrase or symbol. Understanding is a powerful thing. It is the foundation of application; application flows out of understanding, and this empowers a person to take action, which can produce incredible results. Definitions give clarity to an outline. I was contemplating the other day on my many years of suffering and failure. I did this to understand more clearly what it was that brought me to a place of success. There was a time when nothing seemed to work for me, in fact, almost everything appeared to be working against me. I made the connection that reading and studying was my way of escape, and I am not talking about getting an education to get a job. I began reading a lot of books on personal development and I attended many workshops and seminars. These are also my inspiration and motivation to write as many books as possible in my life time that can help many to succeed in life. I want to die empty!

Potential means…

- A possibility that exists.
- The inherent capacity for coming into being.
- You are more than what you are right now.
- It means dormant power and abilities.
- It means un-used power and abilities.
- It means unused success, prosperity and wealth.
- You can do things that you can't imagine.
- You can live your best life and have the best in this life.

My understanding of what potential is and how it works has changed my life. I am now an achiever, something I previously only admired in others. Nevertheless, I am grateful that I did not start out being an achiever. We learn far more from our failure than success. This does not mean you should fail all the time to learn something new. Be wise enough to also learn from other people's failure. Furthermore, do not fail at the same thing more than once; make new mistakes. Failure has produced great compassion in me for those who fail in life and my past keeps me humble. However, it is the meek who will inherit the earth, simply because the arrogant tend to lose what they have; actually, it gets transferred to the meek. I have a few things that I do to keep myself humble. What do you do to keep yourself humble?

HOW DOES POTENTIAL WORK?

Potential operates just like the economic system of the world. It is based on demand and supply – the greater the demand the greater the potential to produce more to keep up with the supply, which leads to greater profit. We all have a great supply of power and abilities that lie dormant within us. The only way for this potential to come forth is to place a demand on your potential. A demand can be a challenge, an obstacle, a problem, a monthly target that you must reach, or a challenging vision, mission or goal and intense pressure. How one responds to any of these will determine the release of one's potential. Being negative, complaining and murmuring is a sure way to sabotage this potential. Nonetheless, that is the reaction of many people in this world. No wonder there are more failures than successes in this world. Learn to confront what confronts you. We rob ourselves from releasing our potential and we weaken ourselves when we shy away from challenges.

On the contrary, people who respond positively and passionately to any kind of demand find great access in the potential to supply whatever is necessary to achieve and accomplish their goals. Most of the time this leads to the discovery of hidden strengths, talents and abilities; even our weaknesses and shortcomings can be revealed to us, which can lead to further development. People who are self-motivated constantly challenge themselves to achieve more and more. Nonetheless, self-motivation is the ideal goal for those who are not yet self-motivated, which means you need to find yourself a coach or a mentor to challenge you to do what you would have never otherwise done on your own. You need this to develop a sense of self-motivation. Forget about starting a business if you are not yet self-motivated. You still need a job, so that you can be challenged by your group leader, supervisor or manager until you can make a deep inner connection of the importance of self-motivation. You cannot maximize your potential without motivation or self-motivation. Without motivation, we all tend to take the path of least effort. Laziness is an addiction - it is the drug of many in this world. Laziness is the enemy of potential.

POTENTIAL CAN BE LIKENED TO GOLD DIGGING:

Your potential is your gold. You don't need money to succeed; your potential supply to the demands of life will bring you lots of money. To get gold out of the earth a miner needs to put forth energy, effort, skill, time and wisdom, and eventually he will be richly rewarded for his attention and patience.

Human potential works exactly like gold digging. You need to put forth energy, effort, skill, time, knowledge and wisdom to achieve your goals. You need to set yourself challenging goals to push yourself to do research, ask questions, read more, take action, etc., to tap from your human potential thus releasing your potential to keep up with the demands of your challenging goals. Every goal that you achieve will be a measure of potential that you release. This released potential then becomes a natural ability that will help you to release more potential in the future. In this whole process, you will also begin to improve your self-confidence and self-esteem, which will increase your success energy. The greater your success energy the easier it becomes to maximize your potential until you become a peak performer and an achiever in this world.

How much we have achieved and accomplished in our lives is an outer sign of how much of our inner potential we have released. What has been your greatest challenge in life? How well did you respond to it. My greatest challenge in life has been my desire not to work in some eight hour job every day of my life. This is not how I wanted to make my money. How I would achieve this goal was a challenge far beyond my current means at that time. I could hardly imagine how I would make it happen. Doubtless to say, I had to fight deep insecurities, past failure, fear, feelings of inadequacies and insignificance. These were my inner enemies that were standing between me and my great untapped potential. Thank God my determination was stronger than these disempowering emotions. Feeling powerless is a terrible feeling, yet it is also a big lie, because none of us is really powerless, we have dormant power – a power that makes us feel powerless at the time and which requires great inner strength and capacity to tap from. Negative feelings and emotions cripple our inner strength and capacity which we need to be able to draw from our power.

Nevertheless, I did finish my daytime eight hour job, and I had the privilege of firing my boss by resigning. I now live for what I am wired for, and I have three types of income to sustain my lifestyle. I am working to fulfil my life's calling, which is to write and to speak. This did not happen overnight – there was an intense process between me quitting my daytime work and the life I wanted to live.

Another great challenge was my desire to successfully convert my salary income into passive income and portfolio income. This great challenge has released and maximized much of my potential and I am now so thankful that I was willing to take on the giant-like challenge. I have a network marketing business that buys my investments every month, which is both passive and portfolio income; and I also, have rental properties that are another form of passive income. All things are possible to those who believe wholeheartedly that all things are indeed possible. What are the giants in your life that tell you that you can't do what you want to do?

Set yourself some real challenging goals and see how you can break them up into manageable sizes and begin to take some positive action towards them. Just finding out about your goals is real positive action that can spin off some energy that can empower you to take greater action steps. This is the way to discover who you really are. You are far more than what you think you are. I am not sure who said it, but there is a worthwhile saying; 'Your potential is a gift from your Creator and what you do with your potential is your gift to your Creator'. I think it makes real sense to think about the gift you want to offer to the One who was so extremely generous to you, giving you so much power to achieve whatever you set your mind on.

Chapter 4

You and your heart

I am not referring to the hollow muscular organ located behind the sternum and between the lungs. I am referring to the locus of feelings and intuition. I like to call it your 'knower'. In your heart you know what is true. A heart person is one who has an ability to express the affection he or she feels. A mind person finds it very hard to express his or her emotions and affections, which can be very frustrating to a heart person.

What are you - a heart or mind person? We have to develop both the heart and mind to become an effective person in this world. Mind people have an ability to take action to get things done. This is not the case with heart people. They are slow to take action, but are also more tolerant and patient with others; mind people are very intolerant and impatient.

This chapter deals with your heart, which is the place where life flows from. What we say and do reveals the issues that are in our heart, because out of the abundance of the heart the mouth speaks. It is important to know that our hearts are capable of extreme wickedness; we do not really know its content. What we say and do reveals to us and others what is really in our heart. Our life's circumstances are also a mirror reflection of what is in our heart, and the issues in our heart eventually become our life's circumstances.

'Circumstances' is a word that is made up of the two words. 'Circle' plus 'stance' (stand) equals 'circumstance'. You are the one standing in the circle; whatever is in the circle is what comes from your heart. We are by nature; circumstance creators, therefore we are one hundred percent responsible for our lives – we have no one to blame, except for events beyond our control. You are not responsible for the wind that blows off your house rooftop, but it is in your power to fix the roof. You cannot help if it rains, but it is in your power to get an umbrella. Blaming and accusing others strips us of our personal power, which is an ability to get things done. We must learn to take responsibility for what happens to us irrespective of who is right or wrong. This is empowering living that makes us become wiser, stronger and stable.

Our heart can be likened to a bank account. Whatever happens to us in life becomes a deposit. Negative life experiences become negative deposits; positive life experiences are positive deposits. The demands that life places on us at times can be likened to withdrawals, which result in a reaction or response. What is the difference between a reaction and a response? A reaction is a negative attitude, because of a negative experience. A response is a positive attitude in the heat of the moment because of a positive good life experience.

A reaction releases negative energy that makes the situation become worse. A response releases positive energy that helps to resolve a matter positively. Who we really are becomes evident when we are under pressure. Every event in life gives us an opportunity to assess the issues in our hearts. It also gives us an opportunity to cleanse our hearts from the negative life experiences that we had in times past.

There are three gates that give access to our heart. These three gates are: 'mouth gate', 'eye gate' and 'ear gate'. Whatever we say with our mouths gets into our heart. Whatever we hear with our ears gets into our heart. Whatever we see with our eyes gets into our heart.

Your heart is your greatest asset. Look after it well, lest it becomes your greatest liability. Guard your heart above all things, because out of it flow the issues of life that creates your life's circumstance. You know how it feels when someone makes you angry; this feeling is a heart issue; deal with it as quickly as possible. You also know how it feels when a frustration or irritation enters your heart; deal with it quickly. Get it out of your heart, because it will set you up in the future for some kind of a disaster. An asset adds things to our lives; a liability detracts things from our lives. Let your heart work for you all the days of your life!

CHAPTER 5

YOU AND YOUR HABITS

Habits shape and mould what we become in life and in this world. Our habits form through our daily actions and make us become who we are. 'Habit' simply means that our action is on autopilot and we do what we do, unconsciously. Whatever we do unconsciously controls us and it is a terrible thing to be controlled by things that we are unaware of. Therefore one should become aware of ones bad habits.

I would recommend you read the book of Stephen R. Covey, which is called The Seven Habits of Highly Effective People. My goal with this chapter is simply to create an awareness of some of the things that are very crucial to the shaping of our lives. In this book you will learn about the habits that make a positive difference in our world. These habits can be developed by anyone.

It has been said that habits are formed within twenty one days, if you focus and stay consistent with the new habit that you want to form. In the same way bad habits can be broken down within twenty one days, if you stay focused and consistent in saying no to the thought pattern, behaviour and action that has formed the habit. The first four days of breaking a habit are the most difficult and challenging phase of the process. You are half way through to your victory over a bad habit once you have survived these four days.

I think it is very important that we should become aware of the habits breaking down our worth and character, because our character is the key to our destiny. Our lives will remain unchanged unless we value what we become in life, because being comes before doing. What we become determines our ability and capacity to get things done in this world. Developing value-adding habits is helpful to developing our character. A bad habit does exactly what it says; it makes us become bad people.

Habits start with the kind of thoughts that we think about on a daily basis. Our lives tend to move in the direction of our most dominant thoughts. In order to develop good habits we must decide what kind of quality thoughts we will make our most dominant. We do this through daily meditation, affirmation, contemplation, visualization and reflection.

Thoughts are highly energetic – they create our feelings. Our feelings dictate our behaviour and our behaviour leads us to take certain actions. It is our actions that form our habits and our habits shape our character.

This process has seven steps:

- Thoughts
- Emotions
- Behaviour / attitude / conduct
- Action

- Habits
- Character
- Destiny or future

It is possible for anyone to develop the kind of habits that can produce:

- Success
- Prosperity
- Victory
- Joy
- Peace
- Patience
- Great marriages
- Great families
- Great careers
- Legacies
- Greatness, etc

Become conscious of your thoughts, emotions, actions, habits and character development. This is the most simple and effective way to invest into your future and to ensure the bright destiny that you deserve.

CHAPTER 6

YOU AND YOUR CHARACTER

There are a few movie actors who touch me deeply each time I watch movies where the depth and beauty of character roles are displayed. It always creates a greater desire in me to develop my own character. A well groomed processed character is a beautiful thing to behold. They say; you will never be the same again when you watch a movie that moves and touches your heart strings. Nevertheless, the truth is we live in an age that does not encourage character development, but instead, being rude and swearing have become admirable traits to many of our young people. The truth remains that cultures will come and go, but life principles will continue to stand the test of time. There will always be people in every generation who will fight the cause of the importance of character development.

I have seen many gifted and talented young people in our community who have talents that far exceed many who have already established for themselves a brand name in the market place, yet they seem to go nowhere. Robert Kiyosaki once commented that many of us can make a far better hamburger than Mac Donalds, but very few of us have an ability to sell hamburgers like Mac Donald. This simply says to us that there has to be something far more powerful and important than talent to really make it in life. It takes character to develop both your talent and gifting to such an extent that they become an extension of who you are, and to have people buy your product simply because they respect you.

This world is filled with people who have great talent, but they are going nowhere. Character is the key to our destiny; talent cannot unlock your destiny, yet it can open doors and make room for the person. But it has no sustaining power. When the talent and the gift of the person outgrow them, destruction becomes inevitable. Anything we give focus on and give attention to will automatically grow and exceed. A legacy is a combination of talent, gift and character.

THE CHARACTER DEVELOPMENT PROCESS STARTS WITH A THOUGHT IN THE MIND.

- Thoughts produce emotions and feelings.
- Emotions and feelings produce an attitude or conduct.
- A strong enough attitude leads to action.
- Consistent action produces habits.
- Habits shape and mould our character.
- Character leads us into our destiny.

Our thoughts determine what we become. As a man thinks, so is he. We become what we think about. Thoughts are seeds and our character is the harvest we reap from the thought-seeds that we have sown consciously or unconsciously.

Let's look at some character traits that can make a world of difference in our lives. People with strong character have the capacity to make themselves happy in any given situation or circumstance. I am giving you these character qualities to look at in order to bring about a conscious shift in your life, which will make it possible for these qualities to become a part of your life. Darkness causes us to stumble; light causes us to see what is ahead of us. Consciousness sheds light into dark places and on to blemishes in our lives. It brings about a sense of empowering that causes us to do right.

CHARACTER TRAITS:

Love, joy, peace, longsuffering, gentleness, goodness, faith, meekness, temperance, loyalty, discipline, persistence, truthfulness, honesty, diligence, servanthood, generosity, trustworthiness, integrity, positive outlook on life; there are no laws against these qualities!

In their training, bank staff are exposed to the feel of real money. Counterfeit money is not their focus; rather they must develop a genuine certainty of how real money looks and feels. The Chinese are the best table tennis players in the world. This is their motto: They only focus on their strength, which is their front hand. They are very poor back hand players, yet their front hand strength is so powerful that their opponents cannot match their weak hand, which is their back hand. Don't bother to give attention to character traits that are not so good. Focus on what is good.

Chapter 7

You and your self-esteem

Our self-concept is made up of three critical parts; these are self-worth, self-image and self-esteem.

Self-worth is the price we attach to ourselves. It is worth noting that Christians have a very powerful concept that injects great self-worth. An examination of this phenomenon would be beneficial at this point. Many of us think that wealth will bring us some degree of freedom, however Christians believe true freedom is obtained only through the shed blood of Jesus Christ. To accept that God gave His only son to bear their personal sins on the Cross, fills a Christian with an enormous sense of self-worth!

Self-image is a self-explained term - it is how you see yourself. What is the image in your heart and mind that you have about yourself? The image you hold can be assessed by how people in general treat you and relate to you. People will be drawn to you if you have a good self-image. We teach people subconsciously how to treat us. We repel or push people away from us when we do not have a good self-image.

How does it feel like to look at one of your photos? How confident do you feel to carry a photo of yourself on your cell-phone or wallet? Do you feel awkward when people see you looking at yourself in a mirror? I like myself to bits, what about you? I think I am a smart looking guy and I reinforce this knowing by using my photos for my book covers. I am open-minded enough to share myself with humanity. This might sound arrogant to a person who has a low self-image. Arrogance means overbearing pride evidenced by a superior manner toward supposed inferiors. Why would I want to write about self-esteem to help others if I have a superior manner towards them? It is good to feel good about yourself. I don't appreciate people not feeling good about themselves; I always find myself saying something good to someone whom I sense, feels inferior. I love people, which is something that keeps me whole on the inside. It makes no sense not to love people. We love ourselves when we sow love, simply because a harvest is always greater than a seed. I don't know how I have previously managed to live without the love I now reap from sowing love.

Self-esteem is defined as how much you like yourself. Self love my friend is not wrong as many have taught us. We are also taught to love our neighbours as we love ourselves. Don't you think that it is a contradiction to teach people to love their neighbour and not to love themselves? It is not possible to love our neighbour if we do not love ourselves. You can't give what you don't have. You are not able to give love if you do not have self-love. Self-love is evident by how well we take care of ourselves; likewise, we can't love others without taking some sort of care of them.

We take care of ourselves through self-respect, which is evidenced by what and how we invest in ourselves. It is not possible to respect others if we do not respect ourselves. We respect ourselves when we; study to show ourselves approved, by reading books that can improve the quality of our lives, by attending training seminars, workshops and conferences. These things are a good sign that we love ourselves, because people are generally destroyed by a lack of knowledge, especially self-knowledge. I am confident that you love yourself, because you have decided to invest your time and money in this book. Every statement that makes you feel excited is a statement that is building your self-esteem, which means you will be better off after reading this book. That's great stuff to me!

What causes people to have a low self-esteem?

- Lack of true parenting.
- Not experiencing unconditional love and acceptance during childhood.
- Childhood discipline without a proper explanation.
- Rejection.
- Self-rejection.
- Self-judgment and condemnation.
- Guilt.
- Name calling by parents or friends at school.
- Negative labelling.
- Cutting remarks from insensitive people.
- Not being accepted by peer groups.
- Failing at things you have attempted in life.
- Not accepting yourself totally and completely.
- Faultfinding by others.
- Unresolved emotional issues.
- Unfinished business.
- Unnecessary negative criticism.

- Being belittled in a company of people.

- These are just some of the things that can cripple a person's sense of self-worth, self-image and self-esteem.

The following is actually good news: - you have allowed yourself to be programmed by certain negative life experiences, because (truth be known), you are the original programmer of your self-concept (self-worth; self-image; self-esteem). You are a victim who has been taken advantage off because of ignorance and gullibility. It is in your power to change the wrong that has been done to you. Most importantly, we can't change what we do not accept. In other words you can't reject something and expect to change it. You must accept everything as it is in your life, in order for you to change it. This kind of acceptance is called taking personal responsibility, and results in personal power which fuels us with energy to bring about change.

After accepting personal responsibility for your life, you must then find it in your heart to forgive anyone who has done you wrong, and who has thus contributed to your broken down self-esteem. Remember this: Forgiveness is not giving to the one who hurt, disappoint, reject and abused you, etc. The ones who have done you wrong have moved on with their lives, you are the one who has been left behind. Unforgiveness puts you in a jail; whereas giving forgiveness is a gift of freedom to **yourself.**

So, it is your time and season to move on and to get rid of your baggage. Let's create a mental image of carrying baggage. See yourself carrying ten different sized luggage bags from the car parking area into the airport to go weigh and check-in your luggage. Can you feel the weight, frustration, irritation and anger you experience as you realise there is no one around to assist you? This is exactly what people experience everyday of their lives by carrying all the old baggage of their past. How long do you want to carry such unnecessary weight, making your life such an unpleasant experience? It is really unnecessary – you don't have to do it any longer.

This is the naked reality of life: The people who have done you wrong have been victims themselves. What goes around comes around. They give what they themselves have experienced in life. Seek to understand those who hurt or abused you! Compassion is a by-product of trying to understand why someone does something wrong. This is what people do who want to make a difference in this world. The difference that you make gives you permission to enter and enjoy a changed life that very few people in this world enjoy. Life rewards positive action in a big way!

You too have a choice to pass on what you have received, or to change the cause of events by dealing differently with what has happened to you. You can pass on your hurt, or be cleansed from your hurt and create a brand new life-cycle. Perhaps your parents were incapable of nurturing your self-esteem or of giving you unconditional love? Perhaps they too did not receive nurturing and unconditional love from their parents. We can only give what we have. They might have never heard what I am sharing with you. It is most obvious that you were born to be a history maker; one who is destined to change this vicious cycle to make life better for the next generation. That is an honour my friend. Knowing this makes you responsible to do something about it.

You are the seed of a brand new generation who will enjoy a healthy self-worth, self-image and self-esteem; a generation capable of attaining good success with ease, because they have nothing on the inside that can work against them to sabotage their success. I feel these words, because I had to break the limitations and failure in my blood line. No-one in my family attained success and so I had to do some real hard pioneering work, with the result that many others are now benefiting from my success, also including those outside my immediate and extended family. My success is now affecting a community of people. Accordingly, my success energy has increased tremendously over many years, which causes me to now seize from hard work. Life has become easier for me. That is the reward of genuine service to humanity.

Doubtless to say life holds many challenges for all of us. Without a good healthy self-esteem we won't be able to cope with life challenges. A successful life is really about achieving self-control and emotional ability and capacity to work through the challenges life brings to us. A good healthy self-esteem gives us strong legs to stand on.

Learn to love yourself.

Learning to love 'you' starts with cleansing yourself from unloved feelings and emotions, simply because these emotions will keep on attracting people who have no capacity to love you. The unspoken truth is that the creation of your life experiences is really up to you. Knowing this makes it possible to start this creation process. The law of attraction says this: 'That which is like unto itself attracts each other'. That is the reason you should get rid of your unloved life experiences.

Knowledge that cannot be applied is not what you need. So, here I am to give you some practical comprehension as to how to get rid of your unloved feelings. Make time to think deeply about the people who could not really love you unconditionally, as well as those who made you feel unloved. Write down their names on a sheet of paper and write down next to each name what you really felt during the time you felt unloved by them.

The next thing to do is to find an ideal person that can do a role play with of these people. Then express yourself fully to each of these 'people', telling them what you went through when you felt unloved by them. Make it as real as possible; add strong feelings and words to your experience. In other words, pour out that whole chapter of your life – empty your heart totally and completely. The one who role plays opposite you should listen attentively and then apologise for not loving you unconditionally. They should ask you for forgiveness or for another chance to prove their love for you. You must then forgive the person and then accept their love. Then close that chapter of your life by allowing yourself to be affirmed by the person. Each of these role play exercises can be the beginning of you filling up your love tank.

You now have something to work with. Whatever we use increases and what we do not use we lose. Use this love in your tank and begin to love yourself fully and completely.

Things to do to love yourself…

Love is a verb which means you have to take some positive action to begin to love yourself. Don't wait to be loved by others – you can only attract what you have and you can only give away what you have.

- What physical parts of you do you not like about yourself? Why is it that you do not like a specific part of you? Begin to find confident people who have similar body parts and begin to observe how they feel about themselves. If they like that part of their body, why can't you do the same? There really is nothing physically unacceptable about you – the only thing that is wrong is the way you perceive yourself. Begin to change this kind of thinking and automatically you will begin to change how you feel about yourself. Thoughts create feelings. Learn to love all your physical parts, because real beauty is inner beauty. It is only shallow people who think people are ugly. Beauty is in the eye of the beholder. You also need to verbalize to yourself that you love every part of your body. Do it often until you believe it wholeheartedly. There were some body parts of me that I did not have peace about. Now I think that perhaps loving myself is a little magic, as my body seems to have been dramatically transformed! Love has transformational power.

- Think on the times that you have failed in life. Failure is only failure if you do not learn anything from it. Fail means first attempt in learning. A failure-thought damages self-esteem. You need to recover from this to be able to love yourself completely. Take off the failure labels – rethink the event and see what you can learn from it. You close the door on failure only when you find something positive in it. Learn to employ alternative thinking. Every negative event can be converted into a positive experience. A positive lesson from each past failure experience will boast your self-esteem. Go for it!

- There is no human being without gifts, strengths, abilities, talents and great potential. Begin to think about this and you will begin to realise you have what it takes to live a good life. Dwell on this until you are fully convinced, persuaded and confident; then begin to ask those close to you what gifts, strengths, abilities, talents and potential they see in you. You will stumble into all of these things once you become confident. Confidence always produces results.

- Begin to journal all the small successes and different tasks that you have completed successfully. The problem is we tend to rehearse our failures and mistakes much more easily than our successes. Open a success account by recording your successes, and learning to celebrate all your achievements. This is a tremendous self-esteem injection. Learn from your mistakes and failures and stop thinking about them negatively, focus instead on the lessons learned. Stop beating yourself down – learn to love yourself by acknowledging yourself more often.

CHAPTER 8

YOU AND YOUR MIND

Doubtless to say; your life goes where your mind is going. So many people's lives are going nowhere because their minds aren't travelling anywhere apart from their here and now. Life is not a problem solving puzzle, it is something to be enjoyed. We have to learn to look beyond our current challenges, problems and limitations. Reading good books; inspirational and motivational books are very helpful to put your mind on a new path and to travel across places where the author of the book has already been. You will one day magically find yourself doing what you have been reading about. Make reading a habit and you will see what I mean.

Nothing in your life can really change, if you do not change the way you think. Our life is a mirror reflection of the way we think. We become what we think about, and we also bring about what we think about. What are you thinking about most of the time? Just have a careful serious observational look at what is really happening in your life, and you will see exactly what you are thinking about most of the time. I always remind myself never to say, 'I wish I knew this a long time ago'; simply because the teacher only shows up when the student is ready. You are ready to learn this life changing knowledge; otherwise you would have never come across this book. This also means that your life is also now ready to change into something you have long desired. I am happy for you – please enjoy it and don't forget to share it with someone else. That is the most effective way to increase what you have. The only things that we cannot lose in life are the things we give away. Let's take this a little further by me suggesting something practical that you can do to bring an increase in your life. There are some things that you bought some time ago which you do not use at this point – you are about to lose those things through the power of neglect. Why don't you consider finding a person to whom you can give them to, so that you can receive something new in your life? The things that mean nothing to you mean something to someone else. In this way we distribute good, moreover many other good things will find you.

Your mind can be your greatest asset or your largest liability, all depending on how much value you attach to it. So many of us allow junk to enter our minds as if our minds are rubbish bins. Not being mindful about what enters your mind can turn your greatest asset into a liability. Your mind can therefore work for you or work against you, all depending on what kinds of thoughts you allow it to dwell on. We all understand how electricity works; therefore, we align ourselves with the laws of electricity to enjoy its benefits, yet this same electricity power can also become a curse if we do not use it properly. It can deliver a fatal shock. The same thing can be said about the mind – it can bring great blessings and benefits into your life, or it can be a curse that brings great destruction into your life.

A man who allows poverty thoughts to become a dominant way of thinking constantly attracts scarcity; not enough, just enough and poverty come into his life, because his most dominant thoughts become his reality. Another man might allow prosperity thinking to dominant his thoughts and thereby attract opportunities that can bring many increases into his life. Make it your duty to constantly monitor what you think and decide for yourself what kinds of thoughts you allow in your mind. You have the power to choose, so choose wisely.

Your mind consists of a conscious mind and a subconscious mind. Sub means under, but you will fool yourself if you think your conscious mind is more powerful than your subconscious, because in reality your subconscious mind is subjected to the conscious mind. It is only subjected, because it cannot choose what to think, it only accepts what the conscious mind decides to think about. Nevertheless, the power to transform thoughts into realities is in the subconscious mind. This is the heart of the mind, where life precedes from.

Our goal is to use our conscious mind wisely by making wiser decisions as to what we will allow ourselves to think about. We should then purposely think these wiser thoughts on a regular basis to allow these them to become dominant in our conscious mind until they sink down into our subconscious mind where they can be converted into real life experiences. The most practical way to influence your mind with new empowering thoughts is to affirm them daily. You can do this by following a daily affirmation program by saying these new positive statements over and over to yourself to influence your conscious mind and ultimately your subconscious mind. You can also record your affirmation on a voice recorder and listen to it over and over until it becomes a natural part of your thinking. This is how we can reprogram our minds and transform our lives accordingly.

QUALITY STANDARDS OF EMPOWERING THOUGHTS:

Think on…

- whatsoever things are true,

- whatsoever things are honest,

- whatsoever things are just,

- whatsoever things are pure,

- whatsoever things are lovely,

- whatsoever things that can make you become stronger and better.

- Whatsoever things that can improve the quality of your life.

- Whatsoever things that can make you successful and prosperous.

- Whatsoever things are of good report,

- think on these things only.

Quality thoughts produce a quality person. A quality person is well accepted by everyone and that's how we gain the favor of others. All opportunities in life come through people. People will close doors on you if they don't like you. Make time to think what kind of person you would like to become and begin to create your own affirmations to help you become that person. Keep in mind that your life goes where your mind is going. You can decide where you want to go in life and decide on the kind of thoughts that you will make a part of your thinking. Much of the things that I affirmed over many years have become flesh. I am what I have decided to think. I constantly go back to those affirmations to reinforce what I have become. As a man thinks, so is he. You become what you think.

This kind of knowledge holds you responsible for whatsoever is happening to you in this world. You can reshape your world into the kind of world you want. It makes no sense not to immediately start to take control over yourself and your life circumstances. Cut down on non-value-adding activities and begin to schedule quality and quantity time to reprogram your mind.

CHAPTER 9

YOU AND YOUR SUBCONSCIOUS MIND

Let's talk about the heart of your mind, which is the subconscious mind. It is the place where the power of the mind resides. Power is defined as the ability to make things happened. As I have previously said, the subconscious mind does not decide what you should think; it only accepts whatever the conscious mind chooses to think. It can be called a reality producing machine. It takes what you think and makes it become a reality in your physical world. It manifests the unmanifested.

Can you feel the energy vibration of the potency of the subconscious mind as you read about it? The heart-sore part of this is the fact that this dynamite power works against most of humanity, and very few of us benefit from it. However this awesome power has not been invested in us to destroy us, but to be a blessing to us. It is meant to make life easier for us and to accomplish and achieve many things. There is an easy-to-do-zone for anyone of us to live in and in which to have the time of our lives.

Let's look at an example of how the power of the subconscious mind works against so many of us. I am thinking about an example of a very young girl getting pregnant and having to raise the child as a single parent in a needy environment that is not very conducive for a child's upbringing. In fact such an environment is the brooding place of so many potentially negative inputs in the lives of both the mother and her child. All these experiences then impress themselves on the mother's and child's subconscious minds as the days, weeks and months pass by. The mother never had the privilege to be the programmer of her and her child's life; they have been conditioned by their terrible life and their subconscious minds, causing them to make their limited life circumstance their reality. Never, ever, will they have success in life unless they discover the truth of the power of the subconscious, and begin to cleanse themselves from their negative life experiences by renewing their minds with positive empowering thought patterns that can serve them well.

Success my friend is impossible when you have a failure program that is at work in you 24/7 without you knowing it. You don't know that you don't know. This is the exact place where so many people in this world find themselves.

This is the good news; we all have the potential to become 'programmers'. A programme is subjective to change. Change is the only thing that is permanent – the conditions of your subconscious mind are not permanent. What hinders you from becoming a 'programmer' of your life? You don't have to stay on your old program, seek to find the delete button and get rid of all the junk that life has thrown at you during the most vulnerable time of your life.

This reminds me of the story of a donkey that was thrown in a deep hole. Not realising a donkey was in there, people in the neighbourhood began using the hole as their dumping place – all their rubbish went into it. However the donkey realised he was greatly benefited by the junk; each time a bit was thrown onto him, he simply shook it off and stood on it! The more junk they threw in, the more the donkey could rise above the bottom of the hole until he was able to walk out of the pit. You can come out of your pit by shaking off all the junk that life has thrown at you. True - it is easier said than done, but you have to find a starting place. All you need is time, effort, discipline and consistency in following an affirmation reprogramming program full of new empowering thoughts, to begin to turn your life around and to rise above your life circumstances.

EXAMPLES OF POSITIVE AFFIRMATION:

- I am born to succeed.
- I am very successful.
- I am prosperous.
- I am able and stable.
- I know where I am going.
- My life is getting better and better all the time.
- I feel happy! I feel healthy! I feel terrific!
- I have a gratitude attitude.
- There are so many people who love me unconditionally, etc.

Why don't you begin with these affirmations to get you started. Repeat them to yourself three times per day; in the morning, in the afternoon and as you go to bed. Say it passionately to yourself with meaning, determination and with great conviction in your heart, that it is so. Believe wholeheartedly that it is so, because it is so, therefore it is so, and now it is so.

This chapter is for you! Your time has come to connect with the reality of what your subconscious mind has produced in your life over many years. Let me help you to look at your life with honesty and sincerity. Do you really like what you see about your life? Whatever you see around you (that is, your life circumstances) is the sum total of what your subconscious mind has made of what you have been thinking. Your outer world my friend is a mirror reflection of your inner world (subconscious).

- Do you like the job you have?
- Do you like the neighbourhood where you stay?
- Are you satisfied with your income?
- Do you have investment?
- Do you have a life policy?
- Are you pleased with your bank account statement?
- Do you like the car you drive?
- Do you like the kind of emotions that you experience daily?
- How do you feel about your limitations and shortcomings?
- What have you achieved or accomplished thus far?
- How do you feel about your education?
- Do you enjoy your marriage?
- Do you enjoy your family life?
- Do you have a social life?
- How often do you go on a holiday?
- What places have you travelled to?

If any of these questions trouble you; that is the best place to start. Be upset for at least for a full week and then begin to shake off those feelings. Identify all those emotions and write them down on a piece of paper. Keep this in mind; you have invited those feelings and emotions into your life. You also have the power to put them out. This is what you can do next; find a brick for each emotion and then write the emotion on a brick with chalk. Get yourself a big hammer and beat each brick to pieces until you can't see the writing on the brick. Pick up the pieces and go throw it at a dumping place, then burn the list with the emotions on and say, "I put you permanently out of my life today. Your days are over; you are no longer welcome in my life".

Write me an email and tell how it felt afterwards – kingdom@ aomi.co.za .

You are now ready to start a new life. You can now begin to develop your own affirmation program to deprogram and reprogram every area of your life where you want to bring about positive change and transformation. Who told you that the past equals the future? That is a big time lie my friend. You have the power to bring about change in any area of your life. Don't ever feel sorry for yourself or blame and accuse anyone for what you experience in life. Those kinds of behaviours make people feel weak and powerless. You are not powerless! Convince those who think you are going to become a nothing in this world. Something good can come out of nothingness.

CHAPTER 10

YOU AND YOUR EMOTIONS

You and your emotions are like a world by itself; a world most people get stuck in and never come out to enjoy life in its fullness. It is truly impossible to have true success without emotional success. Emotions simply mean energy-in-motion. This energy can either be positive or negative, based on what kind of emotions you may experience throughout the day. Your attitude, behavior, and action will be negative if you experience negative emotions, unless you are able to manage your emotions and are able to change your emotional state. A positive person is one who is able take conscious and deliberate control of their consistent emotions, which reshape their daily life experiences.

On the contrary people who are not emotionally intelligent suffer daily from the pain of negative emotions (negative energy) that adversely works against them. They are totally disconnected from themselves, which disconnects them from everyone around them. You are totally disconnected from yourself if you are unable to identify what and how you feel in any given moment. Most people are numb when they have to describe how they feel. You cannot move beyond your current situation or circumstance if you cannot connect with what and how you feel and are able to release your feelings to get rid of them. Another event will come and add to the previous one and that is how people get buried in their emotions. All these suppressed emotions then become like pockets of energy that block and choke a person's emotional life. There are more than three thousand emotions, but most people only experience twelve emotions, which limits their emotional capacity somewhat! So is it any wonder most people cannot respond positively under normal life pressures; they need a greater emotional capacity to be able to respond. Most of us are reactive, because we are emotionally weak.

Have you ever noticed how very few people can work with difficult people? It is so, simply because we need to be emotionally strong to work with such people. Difficult people are people who are emotionally dead; most of their emotions have been buried in negative life experiences. They need punching bags and lots of empty bottles to destroy to get an emotional release, but they end up treating those around them badly instead.

THINK DEEPLY ON THESE QUESTIONS:

- How are you doing emotionally?
- Are you able to identify your emotions?
- Are you able to express your emotions constructively without hurting those around you?
- How well can you manage your emotional state and shift your emotional state as quickly as possible?
- How often do you feel negative emotions?
- How often do you feel positive emotions?
- How long do you stay in a negative emotional state?

43

- How long can you stay in a positive state without being easily drawn into negativity?

- Do you have the tendency to blame and accuse other people for your emotional state?

- Do you always walk away with positive life lessons from a negative situation? Or do you walk away upset, angry or bitter?

- Have you ever made time to identify the kind of negative emotions that you experience most frequently?

HERE IS AN ASSIGNMENT THAT YOU CAN DO:

Get yourself a pocket book to record all your emotions throughout the day for a full week. Then analyze these emotions to discover at least ten negative emotions that you experienced throughout the day. Write down these ten emotions and ask yourself where these feelings come from. Where did it start in your life? Don't push for the answers, be patient and wait for it to come in its own time. It normally comes when least expected.

The next thing to do is to get a very, very good dictionary to look up the deeper meaning of these emotions and try to understand them. I have done this with most emotions to be able to counsel people effectively, but I will not give it to you – you must get it yourself, because personal research does wonders. Make it your goal to become emotionally wise and intelligent for your own sake. Furthermore, develop a consciousness of what actually triggers these emotions and among what kinds of people they surface. You will see how stable you will become once you begin to understand your emotions – application flows naturally out of a deeper understanding. Understanding will keep you stable and well able. Emotional intelligence is the ability to comprehend; to understand and profit from your emotional experience – it is the operation of gathering information about your emotional life.

THE MOST DANGEROUS DISEMPOWERING EMOTIONS:

- Anger
- Revenge
- Jealousy
- Envy
- Bitterness
- Hatred
- Rejection
- Self-rejection
- Low self-esteem
- Fault finding
- Self-judgment
- Unforgiveness
- Offences
- Disappointment
- Guilt
- Condemnation
- Hurt
- Inadequacy
- Overload or overwhelm
- Loneliness
- Pride and arrogance.

Honestly assess yourself with all the above mentioned emotions. Make it your goal to get rid of these emotions as quickly as possible, because they are breaking you down on the inside. You cannot expect to succeed with these kinds of emotions within you. It is like throwing rubbish into a bin – you are not a rubbish bin. Ask for help to get rid of these emotions.

THE MOST EMPOWERING EMOTIONS:

- Love and warmth
- Joy
- Peace
- A sense of rightness
- Appreciation
- Gratitude
- Thanksgiving
- Curiosity
- Excitement
- Passion
- Determination
- Flexibility
- Confidence and boldness
- Cheerfulness
- Vitality
- A sense of contribution
- Humility
- Calmness
- Happiness
- Satisfaction
- Fulfillment
- Hope
- Faith

How often do you experience these kinds of empowering emotions? Don't let them only visit you occasionally – experience them fully when they come, and journal your experience in depth to cultivate and nurture these empowering emotions. Keep in mind that writing imprints the brain. In other words make a deeper connection with them when you do experience them, so that you can create a habitation for them to stay for longer intervals until it becomes second nature and then first nature. It is my desire to see you prosper in your emotional life, so that you can succeed in life with great ease. Go for it!

Chapter 11

You and your beliefs

A belief starts with a thought that has entered into your subconscious mind simply because it has become a dominant thought in your conscious mind. It is something that you have been thinking about most of the time. This same thought then produces feelings and emotions within your soul, because thoughts are highly energetic in nature. This emotion then takes on a life on its own, becoming a dominant force within you dictating your action, behaviour and attitude in any given situation. Your action then creates an experience that confirms your thought and so it becomes a BELIEF. Confirmations strengthen our beliefs. Belief = thoughts + emotion + action + experience.

This is how we develop personal beliefs. It feels right for us even though it might not be universally correct. We then go through life experiences in conflict with other people, who do not believe as we believe, or who do not see things the way we do. This in itself becomes our war zone that produces much offence, unforgiveness, bitterness and unhappiness in our lives. The moral lesson in all this is that every inaccurate belief that we have formed over the years becomes our enemy, something on the inside that works against us; moreover, we don't know that we don't know. This sets us up for much trouble, which in turn shakes our lives, eventually bringing us to a place of consciousness. Unfortunately shame and pain is the school of many where suffering is needed to bring us to this consciousness, however once at that point we never ever have to suffer again because of our incorrect beliefs.

The intensity of our suffering reveals the level of our un-teachability and stubbornness. In other words the amount of pain we suffer is what is needed to open up our hearts to be taught by life. Our hearts open when we feel ashamed or feel pain. In this way we see things as they really are. In general we do not really see things as they are, we see them as we are. We can then move to the next level: We now know that we don't know. This stage creates in us a desire to learn new beliefs that can work for us and not against us. In this stage we need to consistently affirm the new belief to make it a part of thinking, until it can create strong enough emotion to move us to action that can produce a new life experience to confirm our new belief.

The above mentioned School of Shame and Pain can be a lengthy process as we wait for trouble and suffering to show us the beliefs that work against us, but it is not the only school that life has to offer. Another name for such a school is the Reproof of Life, which means life's use of pressure, trouble and suffering to teach us moral lessons. There are also schools of humility, teachability and open-mindedness. This means we should become a student of life by learning from every life experience, including mistakes made by other people. Reading books and continual studies can also add to our learning as we gradually show ourselves approved.

DON'T WAIT FOR TROUBLE TO IDENTIFY THE BELIEFS WORKING AGAINST YOU:

- Identify the areas in your life where you are suffering much.

- Identify areas where you are failing desperately in life.

- Identify areas that make you sad and feel down at times.

- Identify areas where you don't get positive results or outcomes.

- Identify areas that produce conflict in your life.

- Stop depending on your own way of thinking and doing things. Seek for higher thoughts which are life principles, natural and spiritual laws. Then exchange your thinking for higher thoughts. Higher thoughts produce a higher kind of life; lower thoughts produce a lower kind of life. What kind of life do you live? A higher or lower kind of life. Your life goes where you mind is going. You become what you think.

WHAT KIND OF BELIEFS DO YOU HAVE ABOUT-

- Money
- Sex
- Marriage
- Family
- Relationships
- Raising up of children
- Success
- Work
- Prosperity
- Poverty

- God
- Religion
- Politics
- Career, etc.

Your beliefs about these things are askew and inaccurate if you do not enjoy happiness, peace, joy, satisfaction, fulfilment, success and prosperity in all these areas of life. This means you have a set of beliefs that work against you. How long do you intend to be your own worst enemy? The short answer is; as long as you are willing to continue with your current beliefs and as long as you are unwilling to seek new positive empowering beliefs that work for you. Let me say it again; things happen to us according to our beliefs. Your life as it is, is the sum total of all your beliefs; your circumstance is a mirror reflection of your beliefs. Show me your life and I will show you, your beliefs. Do your best to live your life to its fullest.

CHAPTER 12

YOU AND YOUR PURPOSE

Not one of us is here on earth by accident. It does not matter whether you are born out of wedlock or within a marriage bond. Whichever way you came into the world is God's exact design, plan and purpose for you. A design, plan and purpose we often discover later on in life. I have never seen my father. I heard that he died. So what? That is the design of my life and I was able to close that dark chapter of my life. I am now well able to help, assist and support those who are also suffering the pain of not knowing their parent or parents.

I am filled with very strong emotions as I am writing this chapter, because I am reminded of how empty life is when our purpose is unknown. You are a wanderer if you do not have a sense of purpose and destiny. This sense leads to experimentation and the longer we experiment the less meaningful life becomes. Studies by Abraham Maslow show that a sense of purpose is at the very top of the pyramid of self-actualization. Never in history has this topic become such an important topic to talk about. There is a deep hunger in humanity to discover its purpose and to live meaningful lives. On the contrary, it is such a powerful feeling to have a sense of purpose and a knowing where you are going.

How do we make a connection with something? We can only connect with what we discover through reading and by doing in-depth studies concerning different topics that pertain to life. I made a connection with the importance of purpose when I read about it. This is the connection that will produce a deep inner search. It is the same kind of search when you try to find a lost document on a computer. Making a connection with the reality of purpose is like pressing the search button; only it takes much longer than finding a lost document. For this reason you will never be the same and you will never ever have rest for your soul until you discover your purpose deep within yourself. The act of questioning yourself as to why you are here is an indication that your thoughts are nudging you to connect with the power of purpose.

You carry your future within you my friend, but you have to connect with your future to manifest it. Please stop searching for things outside yourself, instead develop the habit of spending time alone with you. It is our ego that pushes us to chase after prestige, more money; more friends who make you look good; sex; popularity, etc. This kind of search will make you miss your real life purpose.

Make it your intention to live your life on purpose irrespective of whether you know your purpose for now. Your intention will bring forth your purpose in time to come. You can take my word, because I was the most purposeless human being amongst my friends.

I finally discovered that purpose is really about giving yourself away. That's it. The more you give of yourself the more you discover about yourself and what you are made for. We feel most fulfilled and in touch with ourselves when we touch and impact another human being. This is how your purpose will find you. I am an exhorter, which means that I have an ability to inspire and motivate others. At first when I was doing this I was unaware that I had stumbled into my purpose. I just knew I felt good about myself, and now here I am, writing my fourth book, something I could never have imagined doing and something the very idea of would have drawn laughter from my friends. Nevertheless, finding purpose is equal to finding a best friend who will tell you everything about yourself. Yes my friend, by discovering your purpose you will begin to discover many other things about yourself. As I am writing I can feel these words will do something great in you. There is no other attribute other than a sense of purpose that will ever make you feel a fully functioning human being.

Entertain purposeful thoughts about your life purpose and your thoughts will reconnect you with your purpose. We bring about what we think about. As a man thinks, so is he.

There is something about you that adds value to people's lives. This something is something you do, and it makes people feel good about themselves and it somehow makes a difference in their lives. You need to become aware of this thing – this is the thing that will lead you into your purpose. Become aware of the things you do that make you feel good about yourself, that is the power of purpose at work in your life. Give more of yourself, your time and your effort to that specific thing, it will amplify your purpose and make it become visible to you and others. Please don't rest until you find your PURPOSE!!!

CHAPTER 13

YOU AND YOUR VISION

So many people in this world perish because of a lack of vision. They think they can obtain only that which can be seen, believing it is impossible to have what cannot be seen. After all, how can you possess what you can't see? What most people see is the life they hate, and so they continue this kind of life because it is all they can see. We are supposed to make consistent progress in life, which is only possible when a person has a sense of knowing where they are going. Goals are steps towards our vision; not having a vision makes it hard to set goals. Setting goals without having a vision is like driving to a place you have no road map for.

We waste our time, effort and energy when we have no vision to invest those things in. Stephen R. Covey mentions in one of his books that the best way to predict the future is to create it. So how do we create our future? We create our future by creating a vision for ourselves and our families.

For what purposes do you use your imagination? Please make absolutely certain that you are not one of those people who use this powerful human endowment against themselves. So many of us read in the newspaper how bad the economy is and we use this kind of information to trigger our imagination to look into the future and see ourselves without a job, being unable to pay our bills and suffering lack. That is how most people create their future.

I'm reminded of a Bible story that I was told at school about the Israelites who were promised a bright future. Their Promised Land was their vision, but many would not enter it, because they had heard that giants inhabited the land. They received this bad news, imagining themselves as mere grasshoppers in the sight of the giants. They used their powerful imagination against themselves with the result that many of them could not enter into the Promised Land. The only people that could enter were the people who were able to use their imagination to see themselves overcoming the giants and thus possessing their future.

You have a powerful imagination at your disposal, which you can use to create yourself a bright future. No vision, no future. Without a vision your future will look exactly like your current life. This simply means your current life will remain unchanged for many years, until you create a vision. This is the beauty of a vision: A vision that is real within your imagination, heart and mind, will naturally begin to reveal to you your talents, strengths, potential and natural abilities, since these things are what you need to make your vision become a reality. No wonder so many people do not know their talents, strengths, potential and abilities; it is because they lack vision.

Your starting place is to learn from a corporate vision, this is the place where you work eight hours a day, or from an organization that you are part of. The employment you enjoy and benefit from is because of a man who had a vision for a business that would provide many job opportunities to better our economy. Make time to read the vision statement of the business you work for. Also try to get your hand on their strategic plan and their goals for the company. Then begin to become more aware of what is really happening in the company. Observe how they go about implementing their strategic plan and goals. This will allow you to see how a vision becomes flesh through daily activities, because a dream becomes reality through the multitude of business; and a fool's voice is known by a multitude of words. Always try your very best to back up your many words with visible action. Speak with the intention of taking action not to be boastful about the fact that you have dream.

Your personal vision works no differently from a company or an organization. This means you can now translate your learning and the knowledge you have gained from a corporate vision into your personal vision, as people with corporate experience tend to be more successful than people with no corporate experience. Also apply the principle of writing by making notes of what you learn in the corporate world. Writing imprints the brain and we can only really discover the depth of what we know when we employ writing because it positions us to see what we have learned, which sets us up to increase what we know.

MAKE TIME TO THINK DEEPLY ON HOW YOU WOULD LIKE YOUR LIFE TO BE:

A VISION IS A MENTAL PICTURE OF A PREFERABLE FUTURE – A FUTURE FAR BETTER THAN YOUR CURRENT LIFE

- Set aside quality and quantity time to think about your life.

- Listen to your heart, because your heart knows what kind of person you ought to be and what you really need, want and desire. Side-step the temptation to want things that your heart does not agree on, because you will set yourself up for failure to want things that are not meant for you. Be true to yourself!

- Write down the things that you sense deep within your heart. In other words draw from your treasure house the treasures that are meant to make your life better and more meaningful. Putting it on paper is the first step of bringing those things out of your unseen treasure house into the seen world. Your pen, paper and imagination are the tools that you need to transfer your treasures from the unseen world into the seen world; that is, the powerful visible world of the written word. Here you will eventually see with your physical eyes whatever you have seen with the eyes of your heart. Power makes things happened!

- **Be clear about these things:** The qualities of the kind of person you would like to become; the qualities of your life partner; how many kids you would like to have; how you would raise them; where you would prefer to live; what kind of job you would like; how much money you want to earn; what kind of car you want to drive; what kind of education you want to obtain; what kind of goals you want to achieve; what exactly do you want to do to make this world a better place for everyone; what skills, talents, abilities, life experiences do you have that you can use to make life-changing contributions in the world and to humanity.

- You should then narrow down what you have imagined about your life in a three to four sentence statement. This will then become your directional vision statement, something you can memorize and remind yourself about on a regular basis.

- Then create a vision chart by getting photos and pictures illustrating and making your vision become more real to you. A picture says more than a thousand words. This vision chart should hang in a place where you can see it everyday, so that the vision can speak to you to motivate and inspire you to live a meaningful life with passion. That is the end in mind.

- You should now start where you are and do your very best to live in the NOW by accepting everything as it is and see what you can learn in your everyday life experience. Not accepting things as they are is you trying to fight life. Life always wins. You achieve your vision step-by-step, day-by-day everyday. Every problem you solve and every obstacle you overcome is a step forward towards your future.

Keep your life simple and focus on daily success. Define your daily activities clearly and do your best to achieve them successfully each day. You will accomplish your life's vision line-upon-line, here a little and there a little if you remain focused, disciplined and consistent.

In conclusion: I wanted to write a chapter on you and your mission, but I decided otherwise. I would rather include some practical insight about a mission into this vision chapter.

Life is not a career but a mission. Any career reaches a ceiling, but a mission has no limits, it expands all the time. Your career is meant to train, develop, equip and empower you for your life's mission. A mission is an outflow of your vision. It is your mission that gives legs to your vision. It is a task assignment to flesh out your vision and to make it a reality that will change your life, your family and many others.

Assignment:

Set yourself a goal to clearly define your vision and mission statement in one sentence that will make it easy to recite this statement on a regular basis. These statements are the software of what you want to accomplish in life. It will speak to you afterwards once it becomes established in your subconscious mind and it will give you step by step direction on a daily basis.

CHAPTER 14

YOU AND YOUR DESIRES

A concept that has had a tremendous impact on my life, I found written in a book of one of my favourite authors; he wrote that 'desire' in Latin means 'from the Father'. This to me sounded like music in my ears. This knowledge and understanding concerning a desire has freed me up and allowed me to explore the deep underlying desires of my heart and to learn to honour them. Believe me this has opened up a brand new world to me. However, if a desire means 'from the Father' then it actually says to us that desires are mere indicators of what the Father wants for us. This also reveals the direction your life should take. Even more, the One who gives us desires is also able to fulfil them one by one if we identify them, accept them, honour them and release them into the world. Inherent in every desire is the power for its fulfillment.

Many of us feel suppressed and oppressed by our desires simply because we attach a price to them, and it makes us feel intimated. Doubtless to say, that most of our desires far exceeds our budgets and even our future prospects. This pushes us into a world of impossibilities, which tells us to ignore, suppress and oppress our desires, because we consider them beyond our means. We then make a conclusion that it is not meant for us, and that it is only wishful thinking or day dreaming after all. I am here as a loyal friend to you to lead you out of a world of impossibilities into a world of infinitive possibilities. It is possible to live and dwell in the totality of possibilities. You can constantly move into greater good.

You are relating improperly to your God-given desires. Free yourself from impossibilities, suppression and oppression. These are the things that produce so much anger, frustration, hopelessness, doubt, fear and irritations in our lives, simply because desires are so potent with energy. These forceful energies are being converted into negative energy, because we dishonour our desires, and try to suppress and oppress them. Let this creative energy work for you not against you, simply by learning to honour the deep desires or longings of your heart.

I want to quote something Jesus said many thousands of years ago. Let me also say this: Why is that people get so upset when a writer quotes Jesus, but it is fine to quote what other great men have said? It makes no sense to me to get upset about what Jesus has to say, because whatever He says is very helpful to live a successful prosperous life. I am saying 'He says' and not 'said', because His words are alive; He still speaks in the now. These are the words Jesus spoke to hundreds of people, two thousand years ago, in a busy market place, words that are still just as relevant today; 'Whatever you **desire** when you pray believe that you have received, and you shall receive it.' Let me bullet point some of the things that we can learn from what Jesus says about desires.

- The most effective prayers are the prayers that are based on our desires, because what we desire is meant for us. Other things that we pray about are not really meant for us if it is not a desire.

- Prayer is the key to the fulfilment of our desires, which means we must give voice to our desires. Desires cannot be fulfilled if we keep it secretly in our hearts. It must be voiced. Prayer simply means to talk to the Divine, who is our Maker. It is the act of communicating with a deity (especially as a petition or in adoration or contrition or thanksgiving)

- The more you talk about your desires, the more real and intense it will become. Talk about your desires with your friends, it will fuel your desires. It must become intense to manifest in the outer world.

- You must believe that your desires will manifest or come to pass when you have prayed about them.

- You must truly believe that you have received your desires after you have prayed. This is very possible if you know how to use your imagination by creating pictures of the fulfilment of your desires in your imagination, mind and heart. This picture will make it real to you to receive what you pray for, which means you can now say thank you in advance since thanksgiving is faith in action. It takes faith to say thank you for something that you have not yet received in the natural. It has purely happened in your imagination, mind and heart. Nevertheless, the truth is it has happened somewhere. It really does not matter where, as long as it has happened that's what matters most when it comes to desires.

Do not be afraid to express your desires as often as possible as this will be very helpful in making a deeper connection with them. Your true friends will count it a real joy to listen to you. In fact, that is a good sign of a true friend. True friends want us to have the best in life.

Desire is the first step towards anything in life. You can't get anything in life that you do not desire. Desires are the seed form, and the fulfillment of your desires is the harvest. Jesus also teaches a powerful truth about the nature of a seed. He says a seed cannot produce a harvest, unless the seed die first. Why should the seed die first? The real seed lies in the heart of a shell. The shell must become dry to break open for the seed to be released into the ground, which is the womb for the seed, where it can conceive after its own kind. Apple seed brings forth apples; potato seed brings forth potatoes, etc. A dream house seed produces a house; a high paid job seed produces a high paid job; a nice luxury car seed produces a nice luxury car, etc. Do you get it my friend?

So how do we apply the seed concept to our desires?

Keep this mind, a tomato or potato or any seed does not fall into your lap. It is your duty to firstly find the kind of seed you want to plant, then learn how to plant it, and when to plant it. Then you must also learn how to look after your seed. In the same way, you must first come into contact with your desires before you can plant them. You must identify and acknowledge the desires of your heart and write them down. You must then describe them very accurately in clearly defined words that are easy to repeat to yourself. Carry this list with you all the time and look at it when you have to wait in a line or when you sit in the toilet, so that you can develop a deep inner connection with your heart felt desires.

Envisage the fulfillment of your desires until they become a clear colourful picture that is more real than your breath. Only then are you ready to apply the words of Jesus. Release this list of desires into the universe, let it go, and allow the seed to die, so that it can bring forth a desire-fulfillment-harvest. Furthermore, keep in mind that a seed under the ground goes through three stages. For the earth brings out fruit of itself, first the blade, then the ear, after that full grain in the ear. This implies that your desires are subjected to a development process, which requires patience and longsuffering particularly for those times when it feels like your desires will never ever come to pass. It is during these times that you should remind yourself to live in the present moment, enjoy life as it is right now. Your desire-harvest is somewhere in the future, don't give yourself over to wishful thinking, but remain in the present moment. Happiness is found in the now, not in the past or in the future. Your now is the seed of your future. Everyday success is what makes your future become bright.

Free yourself from the desire of wanting quick results without following a definite clearly defined process. Life is in the flow; no flow no life. Become a process minded person and learn to submit yourself daily to a step by step action plan that will make your dreams come through. It is in this flow that you will find life. Be conscious as to when you are being side-tracked by what has happened in your past. Get to the root of it and root it out of your life until there is nothing of your past that can pull you to and fro in your now. Furthermore, be conscious about wishful thinking and day dreaming about a better future. Your future can't be better if you can't enjoy your now. Learn to enjoy your present moment until living in the present moment becomes a habit, which can shape your character, which is the key to your destiny or future. One of the most powerful things that can keep your mind and heart in the now is the power of a gratitude attitude. Be constantly on the outlook for things that you can be grateful for, and give thanks. Better still; keep a gratitude journal by recording at least five things daily that you can be grateful for.

You have work to do. Make your list and follow through the whole process until you are able to release your desire list and allow it to die, and then wait for your harvest to come. Don't let the fact of having no money hold you back as you compile your desire list. I am reminded of how challenged I felt when I connected with a desire in me to drive a Mercedes Benz. This seemed so impossible at that time, and I had to work really hard to get rid of all my doubt and my intense feelings of inadequacy. Nonetheless, I stumbled into my Mercedes Benz some years after I recorded my desires. It now feels so normal to drive a Mercedes Benz; in fact, it feels so common to me now. Your desire is far more powerful than any of your doubts or any disempowering feelings. Learn to accept, acknowledge and honour your deep longings and desires. Life is a rewarder of those who believe that all things are possible. You were not made for this world – this world was made for you. It has all the resources you need to make your wildest dreams and expectations become a reality. I have a Kenyan friend who likes to say this: 'I refuse to be small in this world'. Make it your motto to refuse to be small, poor and unsuccessful.

Preparation always precedes manifestations…

CHAPTER 15

YOU AND YOUR VALUES

I attended a seminar many years ago where I was, for the first time, introduced to the concept of the importance of having a set of core values. Many times we know about things, but never really give them our undivided attention. I was deeply impacted by this concept and I was fortunate to be guided in such a process. I went home with a set of core values that I was determined to make a part of my life. I can honestly look back at my life and see how my life has changed and transformed as I was guided by my core values.

Your values my friend are a compass guiding your life to your ultimate destiny. Do you have a set of core values that guide you and help you to make important decisions regarding the direction of your life? Truthfully, the only sure way to have meaning and happiness in your life is to live by your highest values and ideals. There is tremendous power in living in accordance with our values; it provides a sense of certainty and an inner peace. Peace means wholeness and completeness, nothing missing and nothing broken.

That is a description of how people feel, who are at peace with themselves.

Please don't fool yourself by thinking that getting and achieving things in life will make you happy and fulfilled. It is not enough to know what you want, it is also very important to know who you want to be. It is only when we know what we want to become by deciding what really is important to us, that we will have a sense of inner strength and emotional capacity. Your values will create your life's path by guiding you to make certain decisions that are beneficial to you and by giving you the power to take a certain action consistently.

We become powerful when we consistently act in accordance to our highest values and what we believe our life is truly about. Fulfillment and a deep sense of joy come from living our lives according to our highest standards, but this is impossible if we do not have clearly defined values.

Decision making will be hard and difficult. Knowing your values, on the other hand, helps you to get more clarity as to why you do what you do and how you can live more consistently with what is really important to you. We become stable when our actions are consistent with our values. Out of our stability will flow great ability, which is the power to make things happened.

WHAT EXACTLY ARE CORE VALUES?

A value is something that you consider important or that you hold dear. It is imperative to ask yourself important questions. What are those things that are important to you in life? I went through this process for one entire day with inspirational music playing in the background to make me become sensitive and alert to the things that are really important to me. You will never really enjoy happiness, satisfaction and fulfilment if you do not settle this matter of finding your core values. We are often so busy pursuing things that are not really making us feel good about ourselves. Our values are what fulfils us and what makes our life rich and rewarding.

My goal in writing this book is to help many people find meaning in life. It is very heart-breaking to me to see people experimenting with life. Experiment means to try something new or to venture at something new, or the testing of an idea. Not all experimentation is done in laboratories, people also experiment with life, which is really not necessary. It is best to learn from other people's mistakes. Life is governed by principles and abundant life is locked up in principles. In fact, by applying principles and living by them, we can discover real life. These principles can be learned and studied in so many different ways. For instance, just by reading this book you can learn many things about life and then apply them and find personal joy. This chapter deals with the importance of living your life in accordance with what is really important to you. This principle alone can magically change your life for the good.

I am very sensitive when I write, not to spoon-feed people, but to find ways to challenge the reader to get practically involved with the knowledge I share with them in my books. I have an exercise or a project in mind to help you discover your core values in such a way that you will make a heart-felt connection with the power of values. Can you work with me?

AN ASSIGNMENT:

Think of at least ten outstanding successful people that are within your reach. Ask each one of them what their core values are and write them down. Most successful people have at least six to eight values that they live by. Now let's say you have completed the exercise and you now have at least seventy values that you have written down.

The next thing to do is to set aside quality and quantity time to decide on your own values for life. Play some inspirational music very softly in the background. Read through the sixty or seventy values and decide on twenty values and write them down. Then decide on fifteen values from the twenty values and then ten values from the fifteen and then six values from the ten values. Write these six values on a very nice poster card and hang this card where you will see it everyday. Then set yourself goals as to how you can begin to practice these values everyday of your life. Start with one value for one week, then add a value one at a time until you can put into practice all of them for one week, and then try to live them all out every day of your life.

My values have empowered me to become what I am today. I valued leadership and so I have become a leader. I valued raising up leaders and so I have trained and developed many leaders that are now helping many other people to make a success of their lives. I value team-work and so I have developed a powerful team that is working with me on a powerful dream. We have also developed many other teams that are adding tremendous value to other people's lives. And so all my values have shaped me into what I was not before I had any values to live by. Don't rest until you have values to live by!

Chapter 16

You and your attitude

Our outlook on life determines our attitude and our attitude determines what kinds of outcome we experience in life. Our altitude determines our attitude. A jet cannot take off from the ground when it faces downward! (Altitude); it is perfectly positioned to fly when it faces up. The same principle applies to our body posture, which can be a reflection of our outlook on life. Do you look up or do you look down? Your attitude can either be your greatest asset or your largest liability. It is within our power to dictate our daily attitude. We do this by doing our best to think and speak positively about everything that pertains to our lives. It is our thoughts that produce positive or negative feelings. Our attitude takes on the shape of our feelings. Keep this in mind and you will always be in charge of your attitude.

The two greatest attitudes are servitude and gratitude. These are the two attitudes that cause a positive attitude spillover into all other areas of our lives. Things always flow from a high place to a low place. A positive attitude in one area of your life is a high place – it can affect the low places in your life. Low energy levels are the brooding place of a lot of worthlessness, sicknesses, diseases and negativity.

Our tendency is to want to be alone when we feel low. That is our biggest mistake, because things will only get worse when we are alone. The reason we want to be alone is because we lack confidence to be around other people, yet it is the best thing to do. By stepping out of your aloneness you will conquer low self-esteem and your lack of confidence. You will also be able to tap into other people's higher energy levels, because energy flows from their high place to your low place. Keep this in mind when you feel low. Feeling low will affect your attitude badly.

Are you someone who practices gratitude on a daily basis? If, not, I want to invite you into this wonderful world where you can truly enjoy positive emotions most of the time. It is impossible to feel negative emotions such as worry, anger, and depression in the presence of genuine gratitude. Also it is very difficult to be egoistical when you feel grateful. Gratitude disarms the power of the egoic mind. The practice of gratitude redirects our minds away from negativity, pain and suffering. This may sound magical for a person who does not practice gratitude. Nevertheless, it is nothing but the truth.

The truth is we all have a reason to be grateful for something each day of our lives. Our minds will automatically begin to search for all that we have to be grateful for, once we become disciplined in practicing daily gratitude. Keeping a gratitude journal is a very effective tool to use to practice gratitude. Discipline yourself to find at least three things to be grateful for and write them down in your gratitude journal. Increase it as you grow stronger in keeping your journal.

All the things which we could be grateful for:

1. The things you have.
2. The people who care about you.
3. The love you share.
4. Your state of health.
5. The experiences you've had.
6. All the things that the Lord has done for you.
7. The kind of person that you have become through the transformation of God.
8. The house you stay in.
9. The job you have, etc.

The attitude of gratitude makes us conscious of how much we have to be grateful for. This attitude makes it possible to adopt the attitude of servitude. The only things that we can't lose in life are the things we give away. A grateful heart is a giving heart – serving is about the giving away of ourselves to build others up, to encourage, motivate and inspire others and to be strong for the weak. The purpose of strength is to serve others, not to make us look smart, even though it does.

Serving is the key to greatness. Everything about ourselves that we share with others grows, increases and multiplies. The more we serve the more we grow and increase in stature. We can all become great in life, because we can all serve. We all have talents, strengths, natural abilities and potential. Doubtless to say we all have what it takes to help improve the lives of others and to make this crazy world a better place for everyone.

My encouragement to you is to find your place of service in this world and do your very best to be sensitive to the needs of those around you. You are not too old or too young to become a great person in this world. The greatness of Oprah is a by-product of her faithful service to humanity over the many years.

I also want to encourage you to make these two powerful attitudes your very own. Be grateful and become a servant to whosoever. You will indeed witness how these two attitudes will begin to influence all your other attitudes. Become a force for good. This crazy world needs you very much. Always keep in mind that it is your attitude that determines each and every outcome of what you would ever attempt to do in this world.

Observe highly successful people and you will witness that they all have a powerful attitude that makes them stand out in the crowd. Become one of them!

CHAPTER 17

YOU AND YOUR LIFE GOALS

None achievers are people who have no goals they want to achieve, which implies that there are no tangible things they focus on. A football player can't score a goal if he or she does not make the goal post their focus. Focus is a powerful thing – whatever we focus on we actually empower, and what we empower controls us. It is best to be controlled by something that can work for you. A goal can be anything you want, need or desire.

This chapter deals specifically with life goals – the things that make life run smoothly. Accordingly, I would like to bullet point some of the principles that govern the power of goal setting.

- Be clear and accurate as to what you want to achieve.

- Define your intentions in clear words and verbally express your written down goals to a close friend or two.

- Create pictures of what you want to achieve in your mind, heart and imagination and put it up somewhere where you can view it.

- Constantly keep your mind on what you want and avoid thinking of what you don't want. Tell yourself that you already have what it takes to achieve your goals. Don't be need conscious.

- Visualize your success and feel it as if you already have it. This is called the software of your goals – achieving your goal is the hardware. Everything is created twice – there must first be an unseen creation in your mind, heart and imagination before there can be a second creation. If not, you will become a slave to your goals.

- There are short-term, medium or long range goals. Short-term goals can be any time period from one day to three months; medium goals should be up to twelve months and long term from one to three years.

- Have strong enough reasons why you want to achieve your goals. 'Why' deals with purpose, and purpose is the power behind goals.

- Furthermore, write down a few benefits of achieving your goals – this will fuel your desire to achieve, and it will be your driving force.

- Reward yourself whenever you achieve a goal. Take a friend for a meal or breakfast and ask him or her to join you to celebrate your success. This can help you to anchor your success or bring it home, so you can build up a success energy that will make successes become easy and a natural part of your life.

- Journal your successes to increase your confidence and self-esteem.

As I have said, I have dedicated this chapter for the sole purpose of wanting to encourage you to set life goals. These life goals are the eight areas of life. Success in these eight areas will empower you to achieve any thing in life with great ease. It will make you become an empowered human being who has the emotional capacity to deal effectively and efficiently with any challenge you might face in life.

Failure in any of these areas has a weakening affect on us, it gives off a sense that something is missing in our life. You are not in a good place if you feel this way. Have a look at these eight areas of life and then I want to coach you in terms of what you can do to achieve success in each one.

1. Spiritual
2. Mental
3. Emotional
4. Physical (health and fitness)
5. Family
6. Vocational
7. Financial
8. Social

Strategies for achieving success in the eight areas of life:

- First assess yourself as to how well you do in life in all of these eight areas. Be nakedly honest. In what areas do you suffer emotionally, mentally, physically? What are the needs and wants that you suffer in these areas? Are you successful or do you fail in any of these areas? What do other people say about these eight areas of your life – people's comments are helpful feedback to us.

- Check the kinds of beliefs that you have concerning these eight areas. Keeping in mind that our beliefs can either work for us or against us. If your beliefs do not seem to produce any fruit or results, then you need to bounce things off others who are doing well. Be willing to change your beliefs by adopting new ones that can empower you and work for you.

- Get yourself books or teachings that deal with these eight areas of life. These will renew your mind, because our lives go in the direction of our most dominant thoughts. A new mindset in an area of life produces new results. Make sure that your dominant thoughts concerning these areas of your life are empowering thought patterns. Your thoughts also produce the kind of emotions you will experience in each of these areas.

- Engage yourself in conversations, talks and debates to improve your understanding concerning these eight areas. The more we know, the more we grow and the more we grow, the more confident we become. Confidence is the key to incredible results.

- Set goals for each of these eight areas to take your life to another level or dimension. Read through these goals on a regular basis to imprint them upon your heart, brain and mind.

- Make a daily to-do-list about the things that you will do each day to give attention to all these eight areas.

A false balance is an abomination – it really affects us negatively. Problem solving and finding creative solutions for any situation in your life becomes easy and enjoyable when you have balance in your life. Go check this website to do a test as to how balanced your life is: www.markchironna.co.za. What meaningful life does a person live if he or she makes million of dollars, but has a broken relationship with their partner and kids? Go for balance!

Chapter 18

You and your family

A family consists of parents, their children and extended family members. I trust that this chapter will service your family life with a renewed sense of commitment.

The truth of the matter is we all have some degree of dysfunction in our family. It is also true that dysfunctional families are increasing in our society, which is making this world crazier! Dysfunctional behaviour is behavior that flows from our pain, hurt, rejection, unforgiveness, low esteem, offences and bitterness. Through this behaviour we tend to pass on our past to the new generation. We all have some degree of unfinished business and unresolved issues that have crept into our tissues, and which now need resolution to create a better life for ourselves and those to whom we are related. We should all be determined to close old rotten chapters in our lives by bringing a sense of closure to our past through problem solving. Communication and openness has the power to make right what is wrong.

Husbands and wives should submit to one another. Submission simply means this: 'Sub' means under and 'mission' means assignment. Submission therefore means to submit to an assignment. We submit to an assignment by acknowledging each others' strengths, gifts, talents and abilities. Acknowledge your partner's strengths, gifts, talents and abilities and receive what he or she has to give. Submission is not as ugly as it may sound. It is a beautiful thing to see a couple submitting to one another. Submission is only hard when a couple do not know and understand their life's assignment. I am a strong leader and my wife is a strong manager. She has tremendous capacity for detail (content) and I have a strong ability to see the big picture (context). She needs me to show her the big picture of where our life is going and I need her capacity to provide the finer details and to control the process that will bring us where we need to go. This is how we submit to one another.

We only have the capacity to lead in the area of our strengths and we need leadership in our areas of weakness. Why do we tend to resist the help that our partners want to give us? This is the beauty of submission: We grow strong in the area of our weakness each time we submit ourselves to other people's strengths. There is a rubbing taking place when we expose our weakness to another's strength. Together we are like iron; we sharpen one another. We become like the people we associate with. That is called the power of association. I therefore beseech you to identify your partner's strengths and abilities and allow yourself to be strengthened by them by submitting; submission is not a sign of weakness, it is a sign of maturity. A person, who knows himself, feels secure when he or she is exposed to those who are stronger. Learn to appreciate everything about your partner. Prefer cooperation above competition.

Give also close attention to the development of your children. Don't let them grow up like trees. Trees need only water; our children need our close attention in every respect. Get to know your child's strengths, weaknesses, talents and abilities. Steer them in the direction of these elements and coach them in the area of their weaknesses. Strengths propel us forward, while weaknesses tend to hold us back in life. Also get involved in the education of your kids. Show keen interest in what they are interested in.

To the children I would say this: Your parents are a gift – they are assigned to prepare you for life and your life's partner. Fathers should develop an honourable relationship with their daughters to prepare them for their husbands. A dysfunctional relationship between a father and his daughter will lead to a dysfunctional marriage and a dysfunctional future family. The same principle applies to the relationship between a mother and her son. Dysfunctional families lead to dysfunctional societies.

In conclusion: Make it your duty and decide on your family values, and model these values to your children. Also define the life assignment of your family and live in such a way that your family will make a difference in your community.

CHAPTER 19

YOU AND YOUR VOCATIONAL LIFE

Life is not a career, it is a mission. The purpose of a career is to develop us personally, to discover our strengths, gifts, talents, abilities and unlimited potential, and to develop various kinds of skills that will help us in the future in our life's mission. Our career cannot make us fulfilled – it is our life's mission that fulfills us.

It is important that we always be grateful for our work and the salary we earn. There are so many people longing to have a job. Always give every task you do your very best shot. Never do what you are getting paid for halfheartedly. Whatever you do in life will become evident to everyone if you do your very best. It is foolishness to expect a job promotion if you are not currently putting your best foot forward at work. A faithful person will abound in blessings and favour. That is a fact. Just observe the lives of those who are diligent and faithful in what they are doing. Laziness and slothfulness are the enemies of success and progress in life. Do you have these kinds of enemies trying to attack you at your workplace throughout the day? If so - while reading this chapter, tap into the power to choose, and choose now to become a hardworking, diligent, faithful worker. The power of making a quality decision is the power that empowers us to do what we decide to do.

A hard working person becomes known to all at their workplaces. Managers appreciate employees that enjoy hard work. The key to your promotion is to develop high work ethics and learn to enjoy what you are doing. Also be willing to do extra work that might not be part of your job description, so that you can expand your knowledge and working experiences. This is one of the ways to outgrow your current job. Life will not keep you where you are whenever you become bigger than your current job, simply because we stop growing once a job is not a challenge to us anymore. Life tends to supply us with challenges that cause us to grow and to become more than we are.

Consistently upgrade your current job skills by volunteering in projects that add value to your working skills and experiences. Be open-minded to learn how the different jobs at your work place interrelate to each other. Increase your value to the company by developing the habit to learn more about your job and the department you work for. Becoming valuable is another key to job promotion.

Also become a dependable employee; don't get involved in non-value-adding activities at your workplace. You are getting paid for eight hours; therefore you should give your employer an eight hour effort and focus. It will make you stand out in a crowd. You will become visible and employable for many other jobs that can enrich you as a person.

In conclusion: Be conscious about the fact that life is a mission. Discover your life's purpose through your vocational life and begin to move towards this purpose. Do not only mind your boss's business, also begin to mind your own business at home after your eight hours at work. You have a gift, talents and other abilities that you can employ to work for you. Don't be like a mechanic, repairing other people's cars but never having the time to repair his own car. Begin to use your working experiences and skills to build something for yourself outside the company you work for, while you earn a salary. NB! Don't ever use the company's working hours.

There is going to come a time in your life when you will become unhappy with your vocational life; this happens when life begins to place a demand on you to fulfill your life's mission. The wisdom is to build a bridge while you are working. Work on what you are passionate about outside your job hours, until what you work on can begin to work for you. This is how you build a bridge to make a transition from employment to working for yourself in the future. It is very possible to build something that you enjoy doing to a place of being able to pay you what your current salary is worth. Only then are you ready to make a transition from employment to self-employment. Leaving your job to go build something from scratch is foolishness – having a job gives you the advantage of getting a salary while you are working on your own business.

Chapter 20

You and your success

You have been made to succeed in everything that you desire; to be, to do and to have in your life-time. Every desire you have is a clue of what you ought to become, do and accomplish or achieve in life. Doubtless, to say that you have not been made to fail in life. Failure is a mere consequence of making wrong and uncalculated bad decisions. The way out is to solve all the problems in your life that have been created by this process of failure. You are a circumstance creator, which makes you responsible for everything that has ever gone wrong in your life; accept the things that you had no control over. Blaming and accusing others for your life circumstance is not helpful, it will keep you trapped in your circumstances. You need power to get out – taking responsibility for your life is the key to personal power.

What is success?

Let's first clear the air concerning your understanding of what success is. Well, if I perceive success as having a high paying job, driving a very nice car, staying in a nice neighborhood, having lots of money in the bank and having all the luxury things that everyone desires to have, but I don't in fact have any of these things, then it means I am not successful. This literally means most people are not succeeding if that is what success is. So what about the man who has a low paying job, is driving an old second-hand car, but is well able to manage the money he gets, looks after his car well and takes care of his family, paying the school fees of his children, who are doing well at school and are happy as things are, without having any negative feelings and emotions about the conditions of their life circumstances? Don't you think that this man is successful? The truth is: A man's life consists not in the abundance of the things which he or she possesses. Success my friend is measured in feeling happy and content rather than dollars and accumulations.

So what is success? Success is energy and energy is the ability to make things happen for yourself and others. There are many things pertaining to life and yourself that have the potential to create energy in your life. You can create energy by using your skills, talents, abilities and life experiences to add value to other people's lives and to cause a change in your community and ultimately society. It is far more empowering to give than to receive. Receiving does not change your life, giving does. This does not mean one should not be open to receive, because receiving is a consequence of our giving. Giving releases energy – this energy will then begin to work for you in ways you cannot imagine and open wonderful doors for you. Discovering and developing your strengths and abilities and sharpening your skills through consistent use also creates energies, energies that unlock ideas and give inspiration for things that we can achieve. All energies carry information that needs to be decoded, just like a memory stick carries data that can be decoded if you know how to use a computer. Successful people understand energies and know how to interpret them. The more energy you have the more success you can have. Did you ever feel the energy around people who are successful? Have you ever felt the low energies around people who are going nowhere in life?

Success was and is meant to be your natural state, nothing more and nothing less. It is your duty to attain success and to make it become second nature until it becomes first nature – a common natural part of your life. True success creates compassion in us for those who are desperately failing in life – you cannot understand success if it makes you look down on people. Humanity is one big family – we should be there for one another. We were not created to compete with each other, but to complete each other. Each person should find his or her place of service. Service is the key to greatness. Anyone can become great because anyone can serve. For example, it is possible for any one of us to serve one to five poor people with decent food at least once a week. Life becomes meaningful when we engage ourselves in meaningful activities. It is even more important to become successful, because it is only success that can make a difference. What is success to you? Define and live it!

DEFINE SUCCESS FOR YOURSELF:

SUCCESS IS...

- To know yourself and to understand how you have been wired.
- Total self acceptance.
- To know and understand your purpose for existence.
- To know and understand your mission in life.
- To pursue meaningful goals.
- To discover, develop and refine your strengths, talents and natural abilities.
- To acquire various skills and self- educate.

- To find your place of service and to make your valuable contributions.

- To be able to love and show compassion.

- To have meaningful relationships.

- To meet all your human needs – spiritual, mental, emotional, family (husband, wife and kids), social, financial, physical (health and fitness) and vocational.

This chapter has enough energy to stir something deep in you that can speak to you and inspire you to go for success. What specific things can flow from your life based on what you have read so far? Don't let this energy wear off; decide to take action. The law of action is a wonderful law when you obey it. It will help you achieve what you could not imagine. I wish you good luck for good success in this world. I failed miserably in life and could not imagine attaining success. This was a painful realization, nevertheless I found my sweet spot in life and I am now enjoying good success. It is possible for anyone who has the will to succeed. Success is about becoming your true self and enjoying being you!

CHAPTER 21

YOU AND YOUR PROSPERITY

Well, you may say to me, how can you say, 'You and your prosperity' when I am not a prosperous person? No problem, I can handle that. I would say to you that your current state is lying to you big time and you believe this lie big time.

Your life is not yet finished. You should not live by what you see; you should live by faith, believing that the best is yet to come. If you live by what you see all the days of your life, you will have what you see. Another reality needs to be created in your imagination, mind and heart to change your current reality. You are destined for prosperity because you have a soul, which is the place where everything starts in life. Prosperity is yours simply because you have this soul. The problem is you most probably lack the knowledge and understanding as to how your soul works.

Your soul is your mind, will and emotions. Your mind has a conscious and subconscious dimension. The power of your mind resides in your subconscious dimension - whatever you believe mixes with the power in your subconscious mind and creates your day-to-day reality. Thinking is like planning your future. Your will is your decision making department and it makes decisions based on what you believe. You will believe the things that you are constantly thinking about. Your emotions are energy-in-motion, driving you to take action based on what you have decided on.

You really, really, really do have absolute power over this internal operation. If you believe you are in scarcity and lack, you will make decisions based on your lack and you will automatically feel lack. What makes you think that you can't change this vicious-terrible-going-nowhere-cycle? Can you create a belief that you have abundance and far more than enough in your life? Yes, you can by repeating this statement over and over to make it dwell permanently in your conscious and subconscious mind. You will then make new decisions based on this new belief and you will also begin to feel prosperous irrespective of whether you have money or not, because a belief has the power to make things happen for you. Things happen to us according to our faith. Take charge of your soul – begin to do deep soul work, which is really an enjoyable task once you truly connect with it.

I want you to journal all your negative thoughts and feelings regarding prosperity for at least two weeks. Then renounce and reject these thoughts and emotions to get them out of your soul. Say, 'I now release these negative thoughts and feelings out of my soul. I don't need them anymore'. Then replace each thought with a positive one and begin to affirm them daily to replace your old going-nowhere-thoughts with new positive empowering thoughts. Dig a hole in the ground and bury your old-going-nowhere-thoughts (the page that you have written on). Your thoughts are intangible; therefore this exercise will make it tangible. I did this many years ago and I am now enjoying the good life. The good life is waiting for you – you have work to do. Roll up your sleeves and start to create a brand new prosperous life for you and your family. Don't ever expect something for nothing. Begin to put forth energy, effort and time to create your new life. No man, having put his hand to the plough and looking back, is fit for the good life. Your prosperity can make many people happy and bring great joy where there is sadness in this world.

There are principles and laws that govern prosperity. You can enter the world of prosperity by learning and applying the laws of prosperity. I will show you two principles, but I want you to make it your duty to seek and search for the many other laws of prosperity.

- Prosperity starts in the soul. One has to plant prosperity thoughts in one's soul for your soul to become prosperous. You cannot prosper in life if you soul is not prosperous.

- Give and you shall receive. Giving is your seed, receiving is your harvest. A harvest is always greater than a seed. This is how you increase what you have. You can't wait until you are prosperous to start giving - no, you should give as if you are already prosperous and in that way you give yourself into prosperity.

In conclusion: You have to desire prosperity and believe with your whole heart and soul that it is possible for you to attain prosperity. Develop an unwavering belief that it is possible to become very prosperous. All things are possible to those who believe that all things are indeed possible. Say, yes to prosperity and call it into existence. I have seen many poor people becoming prosperous. I am one of them. Choose to accept prosperity into your life. Wilfully take possession of prosperity. Believe that your world is very, very, very prosperous and that you have the power within you to attract prosperity. Look up, never look down again. Say thank you for your PROSPERITY and begin to share what you have with others. Sharing will cultivate a prosperous feeling within you. The only thing that you can't lose in life is the thing you give away. Become a big time giver through a daily generous lifestyle.

CHAPTER 22

YOU AND YOUR MONEY

This free world, as we see it now, was a world consisting of two groups. These two groups were the have-nots and the haves or the rich and the poor. It was virtually impossible for a poor person to become rich. It is for this very reason we should all be grateful for the Industrial Age. This Age has built a bridge for the have-nots to make a transition from their poverty state to a wealthy one. People found jobs in factories, which paid them far more money than they earned on the farms. Individuals also began to learn many life-skills and became educated to get highly paid jobs. These kinds of opportunities were not previously available. Now, another Age has also come into our world; the Knowledge Age – this Age has made available to us very insightful knowledge of how the rich have become rich. The chances to become rich are now very vast; far beyond description.

It is also important to know and understand that the Industrial Age will soon come to an end. This means this world will again move back to two classes only – the rich and poor. This wonderful bridge will soon collapse and so the question is: on what side of the bridge are you going to fall – on the side of the rich or on the poor side? This reality will be determined by how you manage your money and your financial life. Money is funny to those who lack knowledge about it. How you relate to money, determines how much of it you will have. Your financial background is what you experienced and observed as a child in your family. The wisest man once said this: Train up a child in the way he should go, and when he is old, he will not depart from it. This specifically applied to money. If there was never enough money or no money to do what was necessary in life then in all probability you would have formed the belief that money is scarce. And this is the reality that will govern you for the rest of your life. However, your mind can be renewed through knowledge and new money experiences. If you think money is evil, it will move away from you, because you are relating improperly to it. It is the **love** of money that is evil, not money, because we need money to build schools, universities, hospitals, churches and houses. But the love of money will cause a person to do anything to get money – the love of money is the root cause of evil.

What is happening in your financial life? The answer to this question reveals whether you are financially wise or unwise. Money is a currency; nevertheless, knowledge about money is a greater currency. If you have the former, the latter will come to you with great ease. What knowledge do you have about money? We are living in the knowledge age; there is no need for you to be without knowledge. Knowledge is potential power, applied knowledge is power. However, how can you apply financial knowledge if you do not have financial knowledge? Have you ever invested in books, CDs and DVDs that can help you become financially literate? If not, please consider investing in your financial education. This small investment is the starting place of becoming rich. The more your financial intelligence increases, the more money you will get. I suggest that you start with the book called "Rich Dad – Poor

Dad" by Robert Kiyosaki. This book is a good place to start. My goal is to remind you about your money and to encourage and motivate you to give closer attention to the subject called "money"; otherwise you won't be able to make it in the world of finance.

There are three groups of people when it comes to the "money game", which is in the financial world; those who play the game, those who are being played and those who are watching others play or being played. Where do you find yourself in this regard? If you owe another person or business money and no one owes you, what does it make you to be; a player, or one who is being played? Well done if people owe you money because of the business that you have built, or the assets that you have created thus far. If you are in debt – you are being played. Your enemy is called Mr. Debt – you better start paying off your debts and stay out of debt. If you have no debt and no one owes you – you are sitting on the bench watching life pass you by. Think of ways to increase your money, so that money can work for you in the long run.

I experienced the reality of a principle that says, **"What you discover brings about an automatic recovery"**. I discovered that at the beginning of all life there was a man called Adam and a woman called Eve. They lived in a Garden called Eden. There were four rivers flowing into their Garden, which made their Garden very fruitful. They did not have to struggle to make a living, they had everything in abundance. This discovery is very important because it reveals to us the true nature of life. We were never meant to struggle to make a living. We too must create many other streams (rivers) of income to be able to live the good life. A salary is not the only type of income, but if you are aware of only this kind of income, this is all you will get, because you can't have what you don't know about. People are destroyed because of a lack of knowledge. I also discovered that there is more than one type of income and this wonderful discovery has enabled me to create "portfolio income", which is an income that you get from the money that you invest, which pays you interest and dividends plus it increases your original investment, simply because a harvest is always greater than the seed you sow. The seed you sow is the money you invest - the money you make is a harvest.

I also discovered that there is also such a thing as "passive income" it is an income that you don't have to work for – it is money working for you. I also entered into this reality through the houses I am renting out and the income that I am getting from my monthly network marketing business and the income I get from writing books. My network marketing business is buying my investment to increase my portfolio income. All of this would not have been possible if I did not have the knowledge of other incomes. Discovery leads to recovery. May my life's testimony motivate and inspire you to become clued up with "portfolio income" and 'passive income". Just hang in there and you will see how ideas and flashes of inspiration will come to you to steer your life into a place where it will become possible to get all the other types of incomes. That is restoration, because you are meant to have many streams flowing into your life to make you fruitful and productive, and to ultimately cause a change in this world. All the best in your journey towards a rich life!

TIME TO THINK DEEPLY:

- How do you structure your monthly budget? Has it become a norm to pay debts on a monthly basis year after year? You need to break this norm and make it an abnormal thing. You must reclaim that money, putting it into savings, thereby growing it in order to make investments, thus bring financial increase in your life.

- Do you distinguish between needs and wants or are you treating both the same? Your needs are what you need right now   your wants are what you do not really need right now. If you spend your money on wants you will neglect your needs, which will lead to felt needs. Felt needs that are not been met, leads to poverty. Stop spending money so unnecessarily. Why don't you save money for what you need?

- Do you have a proposed budget, which is a vision of where you want to go financially? People perish because of a lack of vision. People with vision prosper in this world. Develop a proposed budget and begin to work yourself towards that budget. What kind of budget do you want? Create it and look at it everyday of your life. Ideas and flashes of inspiration will come to you as you consistently look at your new budget. Why are you waiting for more money to create a new budget? You don't need more money to create a new budget; a new budget is created using thinking and energy. This energy is not a waste – it will work for you in mysterious ways. Watch it!

- There are some things in your life that you buy that you don't really need, so cut back on those things and begin to save that money. Think creatively about how you can increase it little by little, line upon line, here a little and there a little, rebuilding your financial life step by step. For example; do you smoke? Do you know how much money you spend on cigarettes per week and per month? That's a lot of money to start with. Why don't you consider stop smoking, anyway it is not good for your health.

Don't forget to invest in financial books to help you better understand money. Your relationship with money is an important relationship. Life is more important than money, but money is of utmost importance to sustain a good life. Poverty is an enemy to humanity!

Chapter 23

You and your relationships

Life is really meaningless and empty without meaningful relationships. No man is an island – we all need people in our lives. We all need friends who can make us laugh; friends who talk about the serious things of life; friends you can talk to about anything; friends who you can just hang out or chill with, without the necessity of speaking; friends who can motivate and inspire you, and friends who inspire a consciousness of spirituality in you. All these kinds of relationships bring a sense of wholeness and completeness into our lives. Our accomplishments and achievements in life mean nothing, if we do not have friends to share them with. Relationships are gap-fillers in our lives. Have you ever been down and suddenly feel lifted up by just being with a friend? Mankind is really like iron; we sharpen one another.

Our lives and well-being are dependent on relationships; therefore we should make relationship a priority matter. It must be treated as important. I am not sure why, but it is a fact that unimportant things get our attention much more easily than important things. Important things must be planned and scheduled. This means we should not treat any of our relationships lightly - we should make time for each other. Relationships works best when there is an element of trust. Trust glues relationships together and keeps them together.

An analogy to explain how trust works in real life:

Trust can be likened to a bank account. We make deposits and withdrawals from a bank account, and in the same way we make deposits and withdrawals in our relationships. We can therefore say that trust is an emotional account. You can feel when it is there or when it is not there. Communication is easy when there is trust, but very difficult when trust is low.

To make deposits into a bank account you have to deposit money, likewise in relationships, trust deposits need to be made, that is, you have to do things on a regular basis that will stir the emotions of your friend in a positive way.

Be quick to admit your mistakes if you make a withdrawal. A withdrawal is a negative action or word that has a negative impact on your relationship. An apology will put back into your relationship what you have withdrawn.

A bank account becomes empty when we only make withdrawals. A bank account that stands empty for too long will be shut off by the bank. In the same way relationship emotional accounts that stand empty for too long will also eventually break down. Avoid broken relationships. It is not good for a person's soul to have broken relationships. I would have not been where I am today if I did not have many good friends. My encouragement is that you should look very well after your relational emotional bank accounts. Make sure you are always surrounded by many good friends.

Consider these kinds of deposits and please add to the list:

- being there when your friend needs you
- giving encouragement when needed
- keeping your word
- being on time for your appointments
- saying sorry when you are wrong
- motivating and inspiring your friends
- giving compliments and praises
- standing up for your friend, etc
- buying your friends presents on their birthdays
- making time to express genuine gratitude to one another

What other things come to your mind as you read this list? You can add to it and begin practicing them. Look for opportunities to make deposits in all your relationships, you can even keep a book of all the names of your friends and write next to them the kind of deposits you plan to make. Trusting relationships are worth having, because you will always have someone stepping up to the plate whenever you need a friend to be there for you. It is not good for people to be alone. No one can succeed on his or her own. It is only a fool who reasons in their heart that they do not need other people in their lives.

There are stages in developing relationships:

Shallow relationships are not worth having. They are a waste of time and energy. You could have invested that time and energy into something else that would have benefited your life. Time and energy are commodities. There are people that add value to our lives and some people that subtract value. Relationships are shallow because of no movement and purposeful progression. Knowing and understanding the stages of relational development gives us a sense of where we are in our relationships and what we need to do take them to a higher level, which inevitably increases the meaningfulness of those relationships. Many relationships break up after a really good honeymoon experience. The honeymoon wears off when it becomes impossible to ignore each other's shortcomings and weaknesses. We overlook these things during the honeymoon stage to maintain the good feelings and excitement. Many do not know how to deal with conflict, and end up dealing destructively with the conflict they experience. There is nothing wrong with conflict; it is how we deal with it that is crucial.

It is more important to look within yourself to see how the conflict affects you emotionally, before you attempt to deal with the conflicting situation. First sort yourself out and make peace with yourself in order for you to establish peace through conflict handling. You can't give what you do not have. You need to conquer the war within yourself first before you speak about what makes you unhappy. If not, you will cause a war between you and your friend.

Relationship stages:

- Forming
- Honeymoon
- Storming (conflict)
- Norming
- Performing

Choose your relationships carefully:

We become like the people we spend most of our time with. Show me your friends and I will tell you who you really are. This is what we call the power of association – friends sharpen each others countenance. We eventually begin to look alike. He that walks with wise men shall be wise: but a companion of fools shall be destroyed. The wise shall inherit glory: but shame shall be the promotion of fools. Going to jail is a shame - bad company corrupts character. Many in jail would never have ended up there if they had not kept company with fools. The kind of relationships that we have can either make or break us. Do not enter relationships lightly – be wise to check people out very carefully. I am not saying be suspicious; but be discerning. If not, it can break you in the long run. Look for friends who add value to your life and inspire, bringing out the best in you. Also do not choose friends who do not value the same things that you are valuing, and who are not going where you purpose to go in life.

Do you want success in life? Then seek for successful people to befriend.

Do you want to prosper in life? Seek for prosperous people to associate with.

Do you want to become wise? Seek for wise people to keep company with.

Do want to become a business man? Seek to spend time with business men.

Do you want to study further? Find friends that enjoy studying.

Do you want to become a no-body? The world is filled with no-bodies; you will find one on every street corner. Believe me no one wants to become a no-body, yet sometimes our choices in life do not empower us to become some-bodies.

I am writing this chapter during a time when I am facing great challenges that can either break me or cause me to have my greatest breakthrough. It is during dark times that we discover who our friends really are. I am now very clear about whom my true friends are. They are the ones who constantly make me conscious that they still believe in me and that I am going to come through all of this. This too will pass. The truth is we do not really have many true friends, yet the few we do have, can be more than enough.

CHAPTER 24

YOU AND YOUR COMMUNITY

The most effective way to increase your success and prosperity is to share it with others. The only things that we cannot lose in life are the things that we give away. This holds the saying true that if you give you shall receive. Give more and you will receive more. Give consistently and you will receive consistently. I beseech you to find a community where you can invest your success into others by helping them to become successful. However, giving starts with giving into yourself, then into our household, then into your communities and ultimately into the nations. Let your life count in a big way.

Life takes on deeper meaning and purpose when we go beyond ourselves by focusing on the needs of others. Oprah is our best example of giving and sharing. Watching her show, feeds and nurtures my desire to give more and more. My one on one community services have led to us establishing a gymnasium that pumps positive energy into our communities. We now have more than nine hundred members in our gym. We should never despise a small beginning, because in it lies the seed for greatness. You never know what your small service can lead to, simply because life gives back to those who give to others.

THINK ON THESE THINGS...

- What is it you can do to make a difference in your community or other communities where there is a great need if you are not living in a needy community?

- What life experience do you have that you can impart or share with others that will make their lives better?

- What life skills do you have that you can share with others to help them enjoy life?

- Can you spot talents when you see them? How can you assist a person in whom you have spotted a talent?

- How can you use your influence to provide opportunities for others?

- How can you share your influential connections with others to open doors for them?

- What are the high school subjects that you were good at and had a passion for? Why don't you set a goal to help at least five kids to improve their knowledge of those subjects?

- What instruments can you play? Find some young people you can teach these skills to.

- What kind of business can you start in your community that will add real and lasting value to people's lives?

- What about a friendship club where people can find support to help them achieve their goals?

- What are some of the other things that these questions awaken in you? Define them and take immediate action to get the ball rolling.

What goes around comes around. We can all send out good stuff, so that good stuff can follow us all the days of our lives. The work that we do in our communities is our training ground for the things that we can export to other nations.

CHAPTER 25

YOU AND THE NATIONS
OF THE WORLD

We all belong to a nation and all nations are interrelated, which forms the human race. A nation is a politically organized body of people under a single government. I personally form a part of the "African nations" – you might be from United States of America nation, the Australian nation or perhaps an Asian nation. As human beings we are honestly very limited when we show an interest only in our own nation. This causes a disconnection from all other nations in the world and an ignorance of the world we live in. A new world opens up when we begin to show interest in other nations and cultures in the world.

A culture is…

- a particular society at a particular time and place, eg: "early Mayan civilization"

- the tastes in art and manners that are favoured by a social group

• all the knowledge, beliefs and values shared by a society.

I personally connect very easily with the blacks in South Africa – we call them Xhosa people. I can easily befriend them, and they tend to like me very much. Their culture puts great emphasis on respecting elderly people; therefore, they tend to respect authority. This brought great conviction and a heartfelt connection to me since my own people are inclined to disrespect elderly people and do not really know how to properly relate to those in authority. This is a heart-breaking thought, because you cannot go far in life if you do not learn how to relate appropriately and effectively to those in authority. Corporations put policies in place to ensure that each employee will respect the authority structures resident within it, since these structures ensure order, success and prosperity.

I have also learned to show a keen interest in the culture of Muslim people, as I feel they hold some keys of success, because many of them succeed greatly in business. Their culture taught me the importance to help, assist and support one another to attain success and prosperity in life. We are much better off in life when we are surrounded by well experienced wiser people. I spent an evening with Muslim people who invited me and my family to have a braai with them. I nearly cried that night because I was so deeply impacted by what I observed as to how they treat one another. I saw respect, honour, servitude, love and much caring for one another. I wanted to cry because the experience weighs so heavy on my heart, since I have never seen such a thing. I once heard someone say, it is impossible to be the same person if an event impacted itself upon your heart in a positive way. I walked away that night as a changed person. This has created in me a desire to get to know as many cultures in the world as I possibly can.

I once flew to Australia, and I had a change-over flight at China. This was another event that impacted me; the security guards at the airport made sure that all elderly people and those with kids stand first when queuing to board. I was also greatly impacted by the order, discipline and decency at their airport. Doubtless to say this kind of felt order enforces respect from whoever enters such an environment. There is no place for crime – the environment itself enforces it. How does what I say in my writing make you feel? You've got to feel something, because of the weight I feel as I write this piece. The awesome sense of difference in nations and cultures brings a message that we can all learn from each other to better the human race, enhancing this precious world we all share.

I have touched base with six nations thus far, and I will soon be visiting a seventh nation. I have been in Australia, Egypt, Uganda, Kenya, Nigeria and Zambia and I was changed and transformed by what I learned in these nations.

Setting off from the airport of Uganda reminded me of the wars during the reign of President Idi Amin. The ruin of wars was still very much evident, and it made me appreciate the fact that I have never been exposed to a war and I am so grateful for the peace we have in our country. Doubtless to say, these kinds of thoughts and feelings of thankfulness would have never entered my heart if I wasn't exposed to another nation. This means my heart has been enlarged by an experience I had in Uganda. The people in Uganda live off very little, yet they seem happy all the time. This is one of their cliché's; "I am so happy". How is it possible to be happy with so little? Most of us have far more than these people, yet we are so often unhappy. What is the conclusion of the matter? Happiness is a choice – you must decide to be happy and you will be happy. We all have the capacity to think ourselves happy. Learn to think yourself happy. It is a powerful life skill.

I was also deeply touched and moved to observe the utter darkness felt during the night-time. It is so dark, you can hardly see anything in front of you, yet these people easily find their way in such heavy felt-darkness. This made me appreciate the fact that we have electricity in our country. Our host in Uganda did not have electricity, and I had the honour of being in a position to finance power to be connected to his house. He could not believe that we wanted to help him put electricity into his house - only the rich people in Uganda have electricity in their houses. This friend of mine became a rich man in a day's time when we deposited the money into his account. He then put electricity in his house and now enjoys what we take for granted. This is a good spot to say, that it is possible for your life to change in one day. The key is to be consistent and faithful in your personal development process. Good things happen to people who work on themselves.

I was deeply impacted by the order and decency in Australia. This gave me the hope and expectation that it is possible for any nation to grow and develop into a place that can be enjoyed by all its citizens. Every little bit of good that each citizen contributes in the communities and nation can make a difference. It can be as simple as picking up a piece paper in the street or helping an elderly person carry their heavy bags. Life multiplies and gives back what we put into it.

I hope I am stirring a desire in you for the nations in the world. Desire is the first step towards anything. I met a friend that stirred this desire in me and I could not believe that I never ever thought about other nations. The best of what life has to offer, comes to us when we go beyond "self".

Nigeria is an over populated nation, which makes it so hard for them to create order and decency. This made me understand why a Nigerian would not want to go back to his nation once he had an opportunity to explore other nations. Business very competitive as you will find up to twenty of the same business in the same street, which makes a very long day as people work from early morning till late at night trying to make a living.

This led to another gratitude attack, because where I live, our streets are still and empty by five in the evening. Traveling to the nations in the world makes us aware of how much we have to be grateful for. It is a terrible thing to take things for granted or to be ungrateful.

CHAPTER 26

YOU AND YOUR GOD OR GOD

There are many small 'g' gods, but only one God, who is the Creator of humanity, heaven, earth, the sea and everything in them. Your God or god is the one you give your most attention to and derive your sense of worth from. Anything that we are deeply attached to has the potential to become our god. Materialism is the god of many; money is a god; your career can be your god; your kids or wife, etc. Your god or God is the center of your life. Whatever is the center in your life might serve you well under favorable circumstances, but can it sustain you during hard times?

A principle-centered person is one who is able to endure tough circumstances simply because there is real life imbedded in principles. For example if your car is the center (which is the thing you give your most attention and spend your most money on), how can it sustain you when its engine is faulty. A car is therefore an unreliable god. What about money? It is a powerful god when you have a lot of it. But what kind of god is it when your bank account runs empty. Money answers all things, but it cannot necessarily buy good health or fix a broken marriage or family or your kids on drugs.

I was not sure whether I should write this chapter simply because religion, which is an imitation of spirituality; has made this beautiful powerful subject an emotionally charged subject. I do not appreciate nitpicking, prejudice or any judgment concerning these matters. I am aware that the subject of spiritual matters can be a loaded minefield! Spirituality is not a matter of doctrine, since doctrine has the potential to make people very judgmental; which self-sabotages the real power of spirituality. A spiritual person lives by principles that go far beyond the philosophies of men. It is these principles that give us deeper insight into life, helping discern and understand not only our own life and circumstances, but also the lives and needs of those around about us. You would have to agree that people, who live in this life-giving humane way, are a real pleasure to be around. They are agents in this world. Have you ever met such a person? They are down to earth, easy-going and easy to please.

Another thing that inspires me to write this chapter is a program that I watched of Dr. Phil, who is a real genuine spiritual person to me. His programs bring tremendous order and decency in many problematic areas in our society. Dr Phil talked about "you and your faith" in one of his programs. I was deeply touched by what he said. He was talking about the importance of sharing his faith with his kids, because he wants them to continue to have a Father when he has passed on. He said that he has introduced them to his heavenly Father, who is the Maker of all things.

It is not my goal to share my faith in this book, but rather my intention is to impart a deeper consciousness of all the important things that pertain to life. This book is a mere kick-start to excite you to find the path in life that can produce meaning and purpose in your life. It would therefore make no sense not to talk about this subject; it would be incomplete without this important subject called faith, and faith is important. Can you imagine not having faith to sit on the chair you sit on? You would, instead, be continually afraid of falling off. And without faith you could not walk down the street without fearing constantly that it was going to cave in and swallow you up! Can you see how really important faith is? And this kind of faith is needed only for the temporary things in this world, but what about the faith we need for eternity, which is a life after this life. What is your understanding about eternity or life after death? These are important things to think about and to talk about. I leave this over to you to pursue greater understanding concerning faith. Seek and you shall find. Knock and a wonderful door will be opened for you. Ask and it shall be given to you.

On his program, Dr. Phil shared that his confidence and sense of security comes from knowing that he has a loving Father in heaven who sustains his life and everything he does for a living. This is a Father to the fatherless, and One who sets the solitary in families. This is hope for the hopeless and for the many that have never seen their father. Can you imagine how it feels not to know your earthly father? I know how it feels, because I have never seen my father and I have suffered great rejection because of this. Now you can understand why Dr. Phil's program about a heavenly Father impacted me so greatly. I want the fatherless to know this - there is a Father who can give you the nurturing, loving-kindness, care and security that your earthly father could not give you simply because he too was not fathered.

We live in a fatherless society, which is the root cause of the many evils and crimes in this world, because these fatherless individuals can be emotionally dead, to the point of feeling it is nothing to kill another human being. We cannot blame them, because the rejection they suffer has killed their conscience, which is an inbuilt mechanism giving us a sense of right and wrong. These are victims my friend; they need to hear that there is a Father in heaven that can make up for what they have lost in life.

Hear my heart, this is not a message that speaks down on people; it is not a message that brings condemnation or judgment. It brings pure hope! This has got nothing to do with what Church you attend or should attend. There are many mean Christians in this world. I am not talking about them, because there are doubtlessly many nice one's too. This is a message that can bring wholeness to this world, so it might become a safe place for all of us. I am simply saying let's care enough for each other by spreading love to the unloved. This is a universal message not a church message. The Universe longs to see unity in this world. You are a candidate to do the least you can to bring about unity and love wherever you can. Our grandparents know such a world; we too can reclaim the world that our grandparents once enjoyed. It starts in small groups that can have a ripple affect. It starts with honoring your parents, brother and sisters and close friends. This can spill over to many others areas in our society. Have you ever seen a ripple affect by throwing a small stone in a river. Did you see the affect of it? This is what I am talking about. Every little bit counts, which includes a smile or a touch.

You are not only coming from your father and mother who have came together to know each other, to conceive you and to give birth to you. Your Father in heaven knew you before your father and mother knew each other. There was divine arrangement and unseen workings of your heavenly Father to bring your father and mother together to give birth to you. This makes this Father far more superior to your earthly father. Don't be deceived in thinking you came from nowhere and that your mother and father made you. You are going to limit your life if you dare think that way. There is an awesome world which you can't see where everything comes from. You need to connect a connection with this reality; it will most definitely change and transform your life for the good.

Your earthly parents prepared so many good things for you before you came into this world. This is especially true for rich and wealthy people. They prepared everything for their child and they saved and invested money for the coming of their children. Your heavenly Father has made what your earthly father has to work for to give to you. Your earthly father needs money to make things happen for you; on the other hand, your heavenly Father does not need money; He has already made everything you would ever need, want or desire. You open your life for this to be your reality, simply by believing with your heart and mind that this is true for you. There is nothing to lose, but only much to gain from this kind of belief.

Please don't be quick to reject this kind of belief. Remember I told you that your heart knows everything – make time to listen to what your heart has to say about this kind of belief. I have so many good things happen in my life without me having to pay a cent for it. I realize I cannot prove this to you, since we do not know each other. However I am sharing all this because I want to help you succeed in this life. There is stuff that you can receive in this life without you working for it, but you have to believe there is a heavenly Father who wants to give you what you need, want and desire. You earthly father would give you anything you need, want and desire if he had the money. Your heavenly Father is not limited in what He can provide for you as your earthly Father is! He has influence over all of humanity – He can create desires in other people's heart to do good to you. He controls the universe just like your brain controls your whole body. Why is it easier to believe that the chair you sit on will not fall, than believe what I am saying to you right now? Simply - because I am talking about unseen realities. The unmanifested wants to manifest through you, but you have to believe. I can guarantee you that these words will never ever leave you – you will again and again think about what I am saying to you. Why? Because the unmanifested has visited you and it wants to manifest. If you disagree, the only thing that you can do is to be upset that you ever bought or borrowed this book. Nevertheless, nothing just happens; this book is for you. Please contact me on <u>kingdom@aomi.co.za</u> if you feel you would like to ask me questions to clarify anything I have said; or to share your story with me.

CHAPTER 27

YOU AND YOUR TIME

Time equals money and your lifespan on earth. Waste your time and you will be wasting away unseen money and your life. The way we spend or invest our time determines the quality of our lives and it reveals our current true nature. Time spent, is time that does not add value to our lives; time invested, is time that can change the quality of our lives through value-adding activities. People who are being labelled unimportant in society get such a label because they view time as unimportant.

The best way to manage our time is to determine our life's priorities and our core values, and then to set monthly, weekly and daily goals to live in accordance with those priorities and values. In this way we can invest our time wisely. The question is; what is really important to you? This is a very important question to answer and to clarify to make your time work for you, instead of you working on things that will never ever work for you. How do you determine whether the things you do are value-adding? You will know this by whether your life is progressing or whether it is standing still.

There are three types of times:

1. Chronos time which is the measurement of clock and calendar time.

2. Seasons – our lives consist of seasons. We all go through winter, autumn, spring and summer times in our lives. It is the dry seasons of our lives that make us strong and powerful if we work co-operatively through our seasons.

3. Kairos time is a divine moment that defines our lives and the direction of our lives. This is the kind of time that can magically change our lives in a split second. For example we may meet an influential person who opens doors for us, bringing about our greatest long awaited breakthrough, simply because we have been at the right place, at the right time, with the right people. This happens when we have effectively managed our time and walked through our seasons.

Let's do our best to connect with these three different kinds of time in our lives.

1. As I said, the best way to manage our time is to live in accordance with our life priorities and core values. Do this well and you will be well prepared for the different kinds of season that you will be introduced to by life, and by the Author of life.

2. To every thing there is a season, and a time to every purpose under heaven: Indeed our lives consist of various seasons that can be pleasant or unpleasant, happy or unhappy. Nevertheless, all seasons work for our good.

- A time to be born, and a time to die;
- A time to plant, and a time to pluck up that which is planted;
- A time to kill, and a time to heal;
- A time to break down, and a time to build up;
- A time to weep, and a time to laugh;
- A time to mourn, and a time to dance;
- A time to cast away stones, and a time to gather stones together;
- A time to embrace, and a time to refrain from embracing;
- A time to get, and a time to lose;
- A time to keep, and a time to cast away;
- A time to rend, and a time to sew;
- A time to keep silence, and a time to speak;
- A time to love, and a time to hate;
- A time of war, and a time of peace.

What specific season are you experiencing now? There is really nothing that you can do about it. You can manage your time, but you can't manage your season, you have to accept what the season has to offer and work with it. The reason for your season becomes much clearer when the season is over, yet living in the now moment can give you a sense of hope that all things will work together for your good.

Some of us are in a season of having no income because of not having a job. You have done everything in your power to get a job, but you can't find a job. It is all right; accept this painful reality, because nothing bad is really going to happen to you because you do not have an income. This season has something else to offer you and to teach you important life lessons.

Some of us might have completed our studies and are now enjoying a season of earning an income after many years of studies. Make the most of your income – don't spend it all – learn about investment and begin to invest a portion of your income.

There are some of us who are in a season of starting a business, and it feels very hard because there is not yet a comfortable cash flow. This too will pass - just hang in there. This season is to build capacity in you to ready you to handle great wealth and abundance, which come with great responsibility.

These are just a few examples of seasons. Be clear about the season you find yourself in and walk the process to get you ready for a Kairos moment that can change your entire life for the good. Also keep in mind that all things work together for our good. We can only discover the good in the bad by looking for the good. Negatives are always very obvious – the good is what we have to look for. Also keep in mind that you are completely healed when you feel grateful about anything bad that has happened to you.

CHAPTER 28

YOU AND YOUR HARD TIMES

There is an old saying, 'There is no temptation or trial taken you, but such as common to mankind.' In other words - whatever hard times you go through, rest assured, someone else, somewhere else, has gone through the same kind of thing. None of us is exempt from hard times and temptations.

Hard times are meant to shape and mould us just like stormy winds shape mountains, or like fire purifies gold. Sometimes hard times feel like burning fire, but look at it this way, it is a fire which burns chaff from our lives. Chaff (for example a bad habit in our lives), is that which makes us less human, by shaping us into the kind of people we are not destined to be. Destiny is constantly at work in our lives to make us ready for a better future. How can the clay say to the potter this is how I ought to look?

Watch closely and you will see that every difficult time we experience in life is from a weakness that has reached its peak and it is now working against us, or a harvest we reap, from all the bad seeds we have sown in life. Pain is not nice but it comes to show us that there is a problem in our life that we need to fix. Weaknesses my friend, keep us back in life; strengths propel us into our future. The storm or difficult time comes to break down the weakness in you and to remove its sting. Just observe yourself after every storm and you will notice that you have become a nicer person, and you tend to be more humble and friendly.

Pain is a necessity, though not pleasant.

King Solomon once said this: Blows that hurt cleanse away evil and so wounds the inner depths of our hearts. A blow is anything that hurts your feelings and emotions. Wounds are a cutting away of something within you that is not good for you. Pain brings deliverance from evil. An onion has many layers; it is a blow for an onion to have its layers peeled away, however as each layer is removed the beauty and purity of the onion begins to be revealed. In the same manner blows and wounds remove dirty layers away from us to bring forth the true you; a beautiful person.

None of us like pain, yet pain is the only emotional medicine that can produce total well being and emotional stability. It takes pain to cure us from the pain we carry for many years on an unconscious level. How many times do we suffer emotional pain and turmoil but we cannot put our finger on why we feel so? Pain is the tool of a personal make-over. A friend of mine said to me sometime ago, that it takes acute pain, which is a temporary pain, to heal chronic pain caused by old wounds. Chronic pain will remain in our lives if we refuse to drink the medicine of acute pain. To drink pain simply means to accept the pain, and not try to reduce it until the cause of it is found.

This is easier said than done, because being negative, complaining and murmuring are all ways we employ to reduce our pain. This is like spitting out medicine, so how can you get well if you are unwilling to drink your pain. This does not sound like good news; nevertheless it is good news because your life is going to be far better after your painful experiences. Just hang in there a little longer. To get water out of a well you have to throw water into the well to cause the water levels to rise. In the same way to get your chronic pain out, you have to throw in acute pain to cause the chronic pain to rise to the top.

Look for positives in negative situations:

There can't be a negative without a positive or a positive without a negative. This is called polarity. There can also be no balance unless you have experienced both. Hard times or tough times are viewed as negative life experiences, yet that is what it takes to bring forth good. Robert Schuller once mentioned that a tough time does not last, but tough people do. All things work together for good, to those who are able to spot the positives within a negative situation or circumstance. You cannot overcome or win in life if you are only mindful of the negative things that have affected you badly. People who come out better from tough times are those who are able to spot positive things and make them their prime focus. This obviously brings about deeper insight and understanding as to why things are happening the way they are. It is this kind of understanding that causes us to be able to withstand testing times. Understanding will keep you during tough times.

- Both trials and tribulations produce patience.
- Patience improves our character and character is the vehicle that can drive us out of the wilderness dimension.
- Trial and tribulation shake loose in us the things that hold us back in life. Keeping in mind that weaknesses hold us back and strengths propel us.
- Trial and tribulation work compassion in us, which empowers us to be there for others when they are in

trouble, to comfort them with the same comfort that we have received from others when we were in trouble.

- Trial and tribulation make change agents in this world.

The naked truth about life is that it is hard at times. It is only when we accept the fact that life is hard, that we can find the inner strength to deal effectively with a difficult situation when it comes our way. Denying this reality creates an inability in us to deal with such situations. There is a high place for every hard place we find ourselves in. To go up we have to go down.

CHAPTER 29

YOU AND YOUR FUNERAL

My goal with this chapter is to provide you an opportunity to reflect on everything you have read. I believe you are not the same person when you started reading this book. We normally make personal discoveries whenever we read personal development books. Discovery brings about recovery by the application of what we have read. Training is all about input, and development is about output when we apply what we read. As we develop ourselves, applying what we read, we can expect changes and transformation to take place. This reminds me of applying linseed oil to a piece of wood. The oil brings forth from the wood, its pattern, which is its true nature. In the same way applied knowledge brings forth your true nature and character.

Knowledge is not power; applied knowledge is power. Power is the ability to make things happen. By using knowledge you are, in reality, tapping into power that can make wonderful things happen in your life. Knowing without doing is equal to a person who does not know things that you know.

I am using the concept of your funeral for you to make a deeper connection to what you have been reading. There is a season to be born and a season to die. I invite you to take a few minutes to exercise your creative imagination. Visualize your funeral. Try to imagine your funeral where friends, loved ones, acquaintances, your colleagues and associates from all walks of your life come to your funeral to honor you. See in your mind's eye these individuals standing at your funeral one by one, to pay tribute to you.

What is it that you would like them to say about your life concerning all these different chapters that you have just read? What qualities of character would you be remembered for, for your stay on earth? What contribution have you made that they would mention? What difference did you make in their lives? Now write down a few sentences concerning each chapter, and then use this information to set yourself goals to improve, upgrade and develop each of these areas of your life. You can then use the affirmations in the final chapter of the book to reprogram your mind concerning all these areas that pertain to life.

Life is for you, not against you! There is an unseen hand working for you in ways you cannot imagine. There are people you will meet that will make a huge difference in your life. Be that person to those around you with the anticipation that your day is coming. Believe wholeheartedly that the BEST is yet to come.

CHAPTER 30

THE POWER OF AFFIRMATION

I want to encourage you to make daily affirmation an essential part of your life. In this way you can ensure you are looking after your mind on a daily basis, because your life goes where your mind goes.

Affirmation is a tool to discipline our minds – a disciplined mind is the basis for developing a peaceful and contented lifestyle. Affirmation can be defined as positive self-talk; self-talk is something all of us do, but mostly in a negative form. Positive self-talk is to repeat to yourself a positive statement over and over (example – I am prosperous, or I am successful) to influence your conscious mind, which can ultimately and through consistency, influence your subconscious mind, which is your powerhouse. The power to make manifest what you affirmed to yourself lies in the subconscious mind. The subconscious mind manifests the unmanifested!

Life and death are in the power of our tongue, which makes us responsible for our life circumstances. We get whatever we say or pay for. What we say about ourselves or our lives can either produce death or life. We invest power in every statement we repeat to ourselves. So many of us say, 'I feel so stupid' and then we wonder why we are making stupid decisions and mistakes. Many of us say, 'I can't really afford it'. No wonder we can't afford the things that we so desperately long for. It is such an important life skill to be able to think about what we are thinking, because we tend to **say** what we think. We then bring about what we think through our powerful mouths. It is time to repossess your most powerful asset (your tongue), which many of us have converted into a liability, and you can do this by making a decision that you will, from this day forward, be mindful of what you think and say.

We can pump tremendous life into our lives through the power of daily affirmation. Doubtless, to say, you will most definitely witness your life improving gradually bit by bit, by day and by night. Life is easy; it is our foolish mistakes that make life so terribly complicated. Learn to use your tongue wisely! Your tongue can do for you what money can't do.

I am writing this chapter to help reinforce what you have learned throughout this book by summarizing each chapter into five affirmations. You can also record these affirmations on a MP3 player or voice recorder and listen to them throughout the day. However, I want you to first say these affirmations for at least twenty one days before you record them. Why? It is wise to first use the power of your tongue to invest life, power and energy into each of these statements, so that your recordings might be filled with life, energy and power when you listen to them. Believe me these statements become stronger and more powerful each time they are repeated. The life, energy and power on your recordings will change and transform your life from glory to glory. This is a powerful way to let your tongue work for you by making use of

127

technological equipment. The technology age is here to serve us in many ways, including making life easier and opening possibilities for all of us. There are some that use it to do evil.

Affirmations – Positive Self-talk

Chapter 1: Let's talk about life.

1. Life is for me, not against me.
2. Life will supply everything I need, want and desire.
3. Life is a precious gift to humanity.
4. I always treat life with respect and dignity.
5. My life is getting better and better all the time.

Chapter 2: You and your life.

1. My personal, private and public life is one.
2. I have a strong sense of personal responsibility.
3. It is never about who is right, it is about what is right.
4. I am too big to blame or accuse anyone for what is wrong in my life.
5. I honor and respect myself.

Chapter 3: You and your potential.

1. I know my identity.
2. I know how I am and I know where I am going
3. My knowledge of my identity increases my confidence daily.
4. I am comfortable in my own skin, because of my identity.
5. I am deeply established in my identity.

Chapter 4: You and your heart.

1. My heart is my greatest asset.

2. I honor the dictates of my heart.

3. I am well able to keep my heart clean and pure.

4. I can clearly discern what is right or wrong, because I know the deep inner voice of my heart.

5. My heart always knows what is truly right for me.

Chapter 5: You and your habits.

1. My thoughts are the starting place of habits.

2. My daily action shapes my habits.

3. My habits shape of my character.

4. All my habits are working for me, for good.

5. I am always conscious of my habits.

Chapter 6: You and your character.

1. Character is who I am in the dark where no one can see me.

2. My character is strong and stable.

3. My character is my key to my destiny.

4. I have an admirable character.

5. I have a deep appreciation for my character.

Chapter 7: You and your self-esteem.

1. I feel really good about myself most of the time.

2. I genuinely love myself, which enables me to love others.

3. I am very unique and special.

4. People treat me with respect, because I have a healthy self-esteem.

5. I nurture and cultivate my self-esteem daily.

Chapter 8: You and your mind.

1. My life goes where my mind goes.

2. My mind works for me day and night.

3. I have a positive frame of mind.

4. My mind is a powerful tool to help me succeed in life.

5. I have a successful mind.

Chapter 9: You and your subconscious mind.

1. My subconscious mind is my power house.

2. My subconscious mind manifests good stuff in my life.

3. My subconscious has been released from all negativity.

4. My subconscious mind is a good servant to me.

5. I know how to program my subconscious mind.

Chapter 10: You and your emotions.

1. I am emotionally strong and stable.

2. I know how to manage my emotions.

3. I am emotionally intelligent.

4. I enjoy positive emotions most of the time.

5. I easily process negative emotions and convert them into positive emotions.

Chapter 11 You and your beliefs.

1. I only have beliefs that work for me.

2. I always get what I believe.

3. Things get done to me according to my beliefs.

4. I know how to identify going-nowhere beliefs.

5. I know how to develop positive beliefs.

Chapter 12 You and your purpose.

1. I am born for a reason for a season.

2. I know my life's purpose.

3. I live a meaningful life because of purpose.

4. Passion flows out of purpose.

5. Purpose is a force for good.

Chapter 13 You and your vision.

1. I have a powerful vision for my life.

2. I am prospering because of my vision.

3. My vision produces confidence in me concerning my future.

4. I have clear cut direction in life, because I am a visionary.

5. I feel very optimistic because of my great vision.

Chapter 14 You and your desires.

1. Everything in life starts with a desire.

2. I honor and respect my desires.

3. I appreciate all the desires of my heart.

4. I am confident that all my desires will be fulfilled.

5. Desire means 'from the Father'.

Chapter 15 You and your values.

1. I have clearly defined core values.
2. I have goals for each of my core values.
3. My core values empower me to make right decisions.
4. I live in accordance to each of my values.
5. I have peace of my mind, because of my values.

Chapter 16 You and your attitude.

1. My altitude determines my attitude
2. I am in charge of my attitude
3. Gratitude and servitude is the best of attitudes.
4. I can't be unhappy and grateful at the same time.
5. My gratitude attitude works for me.

Chapter 17 You and your life goals.

1. I have a goal for each area of my life.
2. I am very excited and passionate about my life goals.
3. My life goals empower me.
4. I am successful because of my life goals that are in progress.
5. I easily achieve all my life goals.

Chapter 18 You and your family.

1. My family consists of my life partner and kids.
2. I have an excellent healthy family life.
3. My family life is an important part of my life.
4. I consider my family life as a top priority.

5. I have unity in my family, which makes us a strong family.

Chapter 19 You and your vocational life.

1. I am positioned for promotion.
2. I am a value-adding employee (business man/woman).
3. I am grateful for my job skills and experiences.
4. I am marketable and diligent.
5. I am an asset to my company.

Chapter 20 You and your success.

1. I am successful.
2. My success energy is increasing all the time.
3. Success is becoming so easy nowadays.
4. My success is attracting more and greater success.
5. I am born to succeed in life.

Chapter 21 You and your prosperity.

1. My soul is very prosperous.
2. Prosperity is an inside job.
3. I prosper in everything I do in life.
4. My prosperous life attracts more prosperity into my life.
5. I am well known for my great prosperity.

Chapter 22 You and your money.

1. I am absolutely ready for big money.
2. Money income is increasing all the time.
3. I have many streams of income.

4. Money comes to me easily and effortlessly all the time.

5. I have a millionaire mindset.

Chapter 23 You and your relationships.

1. I deeply enjoy the people that I am in relationship with.

2. I enjoy the process of building sound relationships.

3. I enjoy making friends.

4. I have many friends because of my friendliness.

5. I value and appreciate true relationships.

Chapter 24 You and your community.

1. I have a heart for the people in my community.

2. I am a community leader.

3. I am adding value to the people in my community.

4. I have community projects that make a big difference in our community.

5. I show great interest in the people in our community.

Chapter 25 You and the nations of the world.

1. I have great interest in different cultures.

2. I am open to meeting people from different cultures.

3. All the nations in the world are one big family.

4. I have a heart for the nations of the world.

5. I am a change agent in every nation on the earth.

Chapter 26 You and your god or God.

1. Whatever I put first is my god or God.

2. Whatever I give the most attention is my god or God.

3. I cannot reason god or God away.

4. Whatever is in my centre determines my life outcomes.

5. There is a Father in heaven.

Chapter 27 You and your time.

1. I value my time

2. Time is an important factor of my life.

3. My time serves me well.

4. I make the most of my time each and everyday.

5. I invest my time wisely each and everyday.

Chapter 28 You and your hard times.

1. Trials and tribulation make me strong.

2. I always try my very best to look for positives when my life feels negative.

3. The University of Adversity is to teach me more about life and myself.

4. Hard times reveal the true nature of our character.

5. I have the capacity to handle any difficult situation.

Chapter 29 You and your funeral.

1. I am here on earth for a reason and a season.

2. I am confident that I will die empty.

3. I am not afraid of dying.

4. I live with the end in mind.

5. I have emptied myself and I will die peacefully.

6. I have accomplished my life's assignment.

7. At my funeral people will speak only good of me.

8. People from all walks of life will attend my funeral.

Chapter 30 The power of affirmation.

1. Affirmations are a transformational mind method.
2. I do my affirmations daily.
3. I enjoy doing my daily affirmation.
4. Affirmation is a powerful tool to help me manage my thought life.
5. I choose what kind of life I want through daily affirmations.
6. I really enjoy doing my daily affirmations.
7. My life is getting better all the time, because of my daily affirmation.
8. I affirm myself daily.
9. My daily affirmations keep my mind in good shape all the time.
10. My daily affirmation is beginning to manifest as a reality in my life.

You have completed this book. Well done! It is impossible for your life to remain the same, because of what you now know. I trust you will remain faithful, disciplined, consistent and optimistic about doing your daily affirmation. I can guarantee success will become your first nature. It is a certainty, if you do your part. Laziness in our lives, works against us.

Diligence will cause you to stand before great men. I am so grateful to those who taught me the power of affirmations; it has changed and transformed me in so many, many ways. I am truly grateful to share this with many others through my writing career and speaking engagements. Set yourself a goal to share this knowledge of the power of AFFIRMATIONS with at least ten people. You will reinforce this knowledge into your subconscious mind every time you share it with another person. This will make your daily affirmations become more powerful, because affirmation works at its best and is more powerful when we have faith in it. Remember what I said: Things in this world get done to us according to our faith, which is a deep assurance that good must come from what you do.

Whatever is real inside you will become a reality on the outside. Any thing that is real is dominant, and whatever is dominant dominates our lives. Let your life be dominated by thousands upon thousands of positive empowering statements that can work for you in mysterious ways. Your affirmations can become your unseen hands working for you in the seen world!

ACKNOWLEDGMENTS

This book is dedicated to my wonderful wife, Yolande, and my two beautiful kids, Jade and Caleb. Thank you for your love and kindness as this book was being written during a very, very challenging time of my life.

I had my trial of a life time and I was writing this book during this season of my life. This work kept me positive during times in which I could have become very negative.

I special thank you to my mum and dad, my dear brothers, Trevor, Clinton and other extended family members who has been a great support to me during this difficult time of my life.

About the Author

Born and raised in Uitenhage, South Africa. He is happily married to Yolande Daniels with two boys – Jade and Caleb. Winston Lucien Daniels has committed his life to the reconstruction and transformation of the lives of those regarded by society as failures and discarded people. His success is shown by the number of people and families having moved to the garden town of Uitenhage, following this vision.

Desiring to make more of his own life, he completed Diplomas in Production Management and Industrial Engineering after starting employment at Volkswagen South Africa (VWSA) in 1987, where he progressed through various job promotions, specializing in the area of workflow improvement. Having resigned from permanent employment in 1999, he was recalled a few months later as a private Consultant, responsible for training and educating of VWSA Employees, Team leaders and Supervisors. During this time, he also traveled extensively to other parts of the country consulting to various companies in the area of teambuilding and efficiency improvement, reducing costs and thus increasing revenue.

While at VWSA, Winston also completed his Pastoral Diploma, after serving as Leader and Trainee Pastor at "His People International Ministry" for a number of years, he was then released to start a ministry in what is now known as House of Alpha & Omega International Ministry.

In 2006 Winston retired from formal employment, which enabled him to dedicate himself to full-time ministry work, and freed him up for International Ministry as well.

To this end, he has travelled to Australia on a couple of occasions, Egypt, Nigeria, Uganda, Kenya and Zambia.

Website: www.aomi.co.za

Email: kingdom@aomi.co.za

ALSO AVAILABLE

Winston Lucien Daniels is also the Author of the following books:

- The Making of Kings
- Achieving maximum benefits through minimum effort.
- The Creators Three Dimensional Strategic Plan and Purpose for Humanity.

Go to…

http://www.amazon.com/Creators-dimensional-strategic-purpose-humanity

http://search.barnesandnoble.com/The-Creators-Three-Dimensional-Strategic-Plan-and-Purpose-for-Humanity/Lucien-Daniels-Winston-Lucien-Daniels/e/9781426927782/?itm=1&USRI=The+Creator%27s+three+dimensional+strategic+plan+and+purpose+for+humanity

http://www.booksamillion.com/product